T0120782

PYGMALION PRINCIPLES

A MEMOIR ON RAISING EXPECTATIONS AND ACHIEVEMENT IN SCHOOLS

PATRICIA J. DIGNAN, Ed.D., J.D.

authorHOUSE®

AuthorHouse™
1663 Liberty Drive
Bloomington, IN 47403
www.authorhouse.com
Phone: 833-262-8899

Published by AuthorHouse 11/05/2020

ISBN: 978-1-6655-0539-0 (sc)
ISBN: 978-1-6655-0565-9 (e)

Print information available on the last page.

This book is printed on acid-free paper.

CONTENTS

APPENDIX

ADDENDUM

Students in our schools are a precious and sacred commodity; only when we revere them can we properly teach them to excel by raising expectations or, as George Bernard Shaw stated so eloquently:

"You see, she'll be a pupil—and teaching would be impossible unless pupils were sacred..."

George Bernard Shaw
Pygmalion

WOODRUFF SCHOOL

Please let Melvin come home for lunch. The police want to talk to him about a possible rape.

This note greeted me the day I became principal of the most troubled **elementary** school in the district. But the fun at Woodruff didn't stop there.

Almost daily, kids were being knocked off bikes with bricks on their way back and forth to school, dogs had boiling water poured over them if they went into the wrong yard, and angry adults were going to neighbors' houses with chains and rocks to break windows or just to cause general mayhem. Blacks and whites lived in separate projects with only dirt or empty trash cans between them, but the air was filled with expletives and language meant to intimidate. Men yelled at the "niggers" playing basketball against the walls of their houses as mothers cowered inside. While the local newspaper was sensationalizing stories of arson and attacks in the "Grove Street Ghetto", the police were kept busy running down crimes against people and property.

Significantly, staff locked all doors at dismissal so no one could come back in to do them bodily harm. The district wanted the school closed and thought that assigning a woman—the first in the district to become a principal during such tumultuous times—would kill two birds with one proverbial stone.

Adding credence, the Superintendent who hired me warned, "Although I recommended you and you were the unanimous choice of the Board, there is such a pervasive locker room mentality in this district you'll never last beyond this school year. Remember, the nail that sticks up the farthest gets the most pounding so do things the way you think they need to be done because you will never get a repeat". Ironically, by doing things the way I thought "they should be done", I was voted President of the Ypsilanti Principals' 'Association—the only female out of 28 administrators 3 years later.

My first item of business was to tell managers of the Ypsilanti Press that since they were exacerbating neighborhood turmoil and unrest while making money off the sensationalism, they had a civic responsibility to help us turn the situation around. Next came city council. I encouraged members to join me on a bus tour of the neighborhoods so they could see conditions of squalor and poverty which needed addressing first hand. Then I named local ministers and mental health agencies to task forces set up to ameliorate some of the anger and pervasive hopelessness among our families. Finally, I went to local businesses and asked them to contribute to our rebuilding efforts any way they could—I told them money, manpower, or materials would all be gratefully accepted. They responded beautifully.

The local pizza parlor agreed to let us host our first parent get-together for free. The paper gave us money for door prizes, and the police arranged for busing for anyone afraid to walk in the neighborhood after dark. Knowing that in the past, parents mistrusted the school based on their own experiences and the experiences of their kids, I made home visits to build trust and ownership. Then I crossed my fingers.

That night we made history! Having been told getting 10 people to a parent meeting was considered a success, everyone was stunned when a hundred and fifty people shuffled in (out of 180 families)! There I stood with my little overhead projector and thought, "okay, we got them but what do we do with them?" This was truly one of the most electric moments of my long career. For the first time, black and white adults were sitting at the same tables eating piazza, drinking pop, and talking to their neighbors. After introducing my staff, I reminded everyone present that we were on the same side and, although we didn't have to agree on everything, we had to agree that the safety and well-being of our kids was our number one priority and we had to quit contributing to their suffering.

We had to, simply, come together, I said.

And come together we did!

Parents volunteered to be on committees formed on the spot including walking the sidewalks to and from school, helping with lunch duty, and being part of a neighborhood watch. From that point forward, whenever we had school functions, it was standing room only! The results were miraculous!

We started a neighborhood network of "Moms" (dads were scarce) so we could build friendships instead of walls. I had coffee hours for parents who were upset about black and white confrontations in the Projects. As tempers flared, I remained seated which helped keep everyone calm during heated arguments. (This simple technique combined with spending many hours in homes and at the school demonstrated my sincerity in reaching positive, peaceful solutions to our common problems and often was all that was needed to de-escalate tense moments).

Although the building had suffered from extensive vandalism, I was amused when the Director of Building Operations asked, "Where did all your bad kids go—did they move? Before you came, we spent most of the district's budget on this building because of window breakage, graffiti and other damage; now we never spend a dime here so we can use our entire budget on the other schools in the district."

I continued to make home visits and started a community school program so kids and adults had someplace safe to go after dark. We offered family roller-skating in the gym, cooking classes in the kitchen, and classes on helping with homework. We brought in agency people to teach families how to budget, and child-care and mental health professionals who offered free counseling. We even offered free babysitting to help make attendance possible. When we initiated "Make and Take" Workshops parents came in droves to get ideas, free games, and materials to create projects to help kids at home.

Knowing that many of parents would never be fully responsible for their own health much less that of their children, (other than through local emergency rooms), we felt an obligation to teach our kids how to take care of themselves. On November 12, 1974, we created a School-wide Health Fair, the **first of its kind in the country.** We had professionals for dental health, doctors and nurses giving physicals and first aid as well as movies emphasizing hygiene or Ranger Glen. We began with a whole week of lesson plans stressing activities focused on health and hygiene, including assemblies where staff dressed up as vegetables yelling "Where's the beef?". Phyllis Mc Donald and Claudia Richie helped develop "menus" for the month. Efforts were so successful we were highlighted in a **national health magazine** and received queries from all over the country for ideas.

Woodruff gained national recognition and was named **one of the top one hundred schools in the country by Phi Delta Kappa** for its improved discipline and parental involvement—a truly unexpected accomplishment, but one that cemented our reputation as a school good for kids.

Once families were firmly in our corner, I knew I had to concentrate on the staff issues I had inherited:

- Previous administrators had thought nothing of paddling or suspending kids for **weeks!** Of course, the staff loved having "troublemakers" gone so they were understandably dismayed when I suggested more positive, inclusive disciplinary alternatives.
- The principal I replaced was loved because he let teachers run the school, hung out with them afterhours, and had an affair with one who, obviously, had not wanted him replaced. Nor did her friends, one of whom was daughter-in-law to the board president, and the other my secretary!
- The head of the local teachers' union had applied for the principalship; when she didn't get it, her animosity knew no bounds. She could be especially dangerous because she was a 4th grade teacher.
- Teachers were afraid of kids and parents who had verbally or physically attacked them; thus, the locking of the doors every day at dismissal. Many staff members were afraid to help chaperone or run programs for families at night. The previous attitude of "these parents don't care" changed quickly to an attitude of "Why do I have to come back to work at night?" Ironically, as more parents came to our events, the more some teachers complained.
- Some of the hostility was understandable. Kids were constantly fighting each other, blatantly disrespectful to adults--even hitting teachers when upset--and capable of all kinds of obscenities, like urinating on walls or spitting in your face if you tried correcting them.

Recognizing that we needed cohesiveness among the adults and limit setting for students, I consulted with a school mental health expert, Ruth Schelkun, and two principals, Bob Hunt and Hayward Richardson, who were already working on innovative ideas for better school-wide discipline. I brought a model back to staff so we could tear it apart then build a comprehensive plan which better suited us and our population. We called it ***pink slipping*** and, within the year, this process had changed our school climate so much that we found ourselves heatedly discussing whether GUM CHEWING should be considered against the rules! Imagine going from fear of being attacked by a student or parent to deciding if kids should be allowed to chew gum…

Of course, by that time the Press was our friend rather than our adversary. When they did an editorial praising my work bringing diverse stakeholders together and having phenomenal success with parent and community involvement, it created a backlash within my staff. The next day, seven women—including my secretary—asked to meet with the Superintendent. When he questioned why they were unhappy with me, the only thing they could think to say was, "Well, she's a woman and she's much too calm and positive during a crisis!" He laughed them out of the office.

By this time, I had hired a school aide, Jackie Bishop, who was young, black and a former student at PEP. Jackie was shocked that staff did not revere me as she did. Extremely loyal to me (at one point she had lived with us), she could not fathom the animosity of the staff toward me and was often more upset than I about the fact that many were still fraternizing with my predecessor. Staff constantly accused me of caring more about the community than I cared about them. Since this had always been their major bone of contention, I began to think that maybe they were right, and I was wrong.

It wasn't until the following fall that I had an epiphany.

At our first-ever talent show with a packed audience, I noticed EVERY teacher was literally sitting on the edge of their seats, constantly looking around --because most of the audience was black. It hit me then: the reason the all-white staff had been so uncomfortable about bringing the community into the school was based on simple racism and fear. What a revelation that was!

Tellingly, members of the "old guard" loved what I was doing and how the community had become so involved; in fact, a teacher 40 years my senior presented me with a necklace engraved prosaically, "Jealousy is the tribute mediocrity pays to genius".

One night when I returned to work through the first-grade teacher's room, hundreds of cockroaches scattered frantically when I hit the light. I couldn't help but think of how much they reminded me of teachers who congregated in the halls to gossip and gripe then scatter like bugs when I approached.

I encouraged those who were still unhappy to transfer—including my secretary, the most disloyal of the bunch—and hired better personnel, more representative of our school makeup and was rewarded with teachers the caliber of Linda Jamieson, Faye Metaj and Claudia Ritchie.

But even the "old guard" were demoralized by constant turnover, tardiness, and poor attendance.

So, I decided to approach the Board of Education for funds to pilot a breakfast program. I knew most of our kids were not getting 3 meals a day which impacted their attendance and poor attention spans. We were the 1st school to pilot a breakfast program and now the malcontents complained because kids were coming even before doors opened, ignoring that both attendance and promptness improved 85%!

Parents who had been most disenfranchised started responding in surprising ways. When I called Mrs E, who had been our biggest complainer for years, and she said, "okay, Honey, thanks for calling", you could have knocked me over with a feather! When Mrs. B. (who had 5 kids in our school) came in one day to tell me, "It seems like I can finally relax now; this school has really changed and you get better teachers every year!" I knew we had really "arrived" because she had never before set foot in the building all the years her kids had gone to Woodruff.

Teachers were making their presence known in some surprising ways also. Some funny, some not so funny. For example, there was "the Donald", so paranoid that some days if you said "Good morning" he'd demand to know why you had "singled him out", but other days if you said nothing, he'd want to know why you "weren't talking" to him. Or Lucey, who said her biggest problem in getting through her day was because she *hadn't taken enough* tranquilizers that morning. Or Terry who had been bitten by a squirrel and was afraid she would turn into a werewolf. But taking the prize, hands-down, was our librarian who landed in jail for solicitation and running numbers in the neighborhood.

On the other hand, it was becoming common to get compliments from prestigious sources and by word of mouth. Eastern Michigan University routinely told people we were the "best school with the best principal" to student teachers, helping us recruit substitutes and new hires. And University of Michigan often invited me to address students in the School of Education on school issues and innovations. I was sought out as a speaker for state and national conferences 23 times due to our dramatic success and the way we always managed to transform seemingly insurmountable obstacles into new opportunities for growth.

Board members started bragging about us to parents outside the district encouraging them to contact me for help with unruly children or homework tips. The fact that I had run Kindergarten Screening district-wide and offered classes in conjunction with the local community college added a special cache to the advice parents sought.

At the end of this book will be tips for parental involvement and ways to help children both academically and behaviorally at home. There will also be a step-by step guide to better discipline that enabled all of my elementary schools to win awards or be featured in national magazines, such as *Executive Educator. Instructor Magazine* labeled our building-wide approach to sanity for students and staff as one of the best discipline programs in the country and challenged other schools to adapt it for their own.

Woodruff always presented its own challenges, but also many moments of mirth. These were just a few:

- A neighbor volunteered to help us with our lunch program but, after his 5th visit, his wife called the superintendent to complain that she thought he and I were having an affair because, "he's over there every chance he gets". When the superintendent called to see if there was any truth to her complaint, I said, "Ray, did she mention that he's 86 years old?"
- Our 5th grade teacher was worried that some of his boys were already having sex, so we brought in the school nurse to teach

them sex ed. When she warned them about sexually transmitted diseases, she wrote the word "CLAP" on the board. So they did! We concluded that most of the talk had been exaggerated and cut our losses before we ended up with a standing ovation.

- One teacher, Phyllis McDonald, wanted to make a home visit with me because her 6th grader was still sucking her thumb and kids were making fun of her. When the mother invited us in, we couldn't help but notice that she was sucking her thumb the entire time she talked to us!
- Another student had to be constantly reminded not to masturbate behind his desk. I told the teacher it was probably her fault because she had kept telling him to "get a hold" of himself!.
- A crossing guard kept hitting cars with his stop sign so a few drivers came in to report it. All we could say, in his defense, was that he took his job seriously, and anytime a car went over the white lines instead of stopping where they were supposed to, he took it personally.
- A drunk came in to use our facilities without asking permission, so I went into the bathroom, stuck my head under the stall, and said, "Sir, come out of there; preferably, with your pants up!" Teachers were shocked by my brazen actions but, as I explained, I didn't know whether or not any girls were in there at the same time.
- We were adjacent to the railroad tracks and, one day, the signal was stuck. When the clanging didn't stop, my community school coordinator, Barb Olsen, called the railway company singing, "Pardon me boys, is that the Chattanooga Choo Choo?" After laughing uproariously, they fixed the crossing within the hour.
- A mother complained that her boyfriend had a gun and was abusive to her kids, so I reported him to Social Services. That night, while I was alone in my office, he barged in and wanted to know which teacher had reported him to the police. I told him I had done it and then lied that I had set up a button to alert the patrols to any trouble that occurred after hours. He left with his tail between his legs.
- Brady was sent to the office for punching another kid. Trying to get him to take responsibility for his actions, I said "Brady, who's

responsible for what you do? Who moves your arms and legs?" He replied, "Jesus". I threw up my hands and said, "maybe we have the wrong person in here!"

- My 5th grade teacher gave me a copy of a letter from Playgirl Magazine, rejecting a man's offer to be their centerfold with the explanation that they couldn't get the panel to stop laughing at his nude photo and wondering if he had hurt himself on a bike or "something". That night a mother came to talk to me about the same teacher whom she felt was "too loose and irreverent". After relating the discussion to the teacher, I asked if she still had the letter she had given me that morning. She said, "No, I left it on your desk". Of course, as soon as I returned to my office, I realized Mom had picked it up with her daughter's pile of papers after we had talked so I had to call her to retrieve it. Talk about being embarrassed!
- One parent did not want her son in an Asian teacher's class. When I asked her why she said, "She don't even speak proper English!"
- We had a 10-year-old special ed student whom we worried was promiscuous, so we called the mother in for a conference. She told us the night before at a laundromat, Marjorie "made a beeline for the scuzziest guys you ever saw". All the way home Marjorie's older sister kept stressing "never talk to strangers because they could kidnap you, hurt you, even kill you." Once home, she decided to see if her admonishments had worked. She said, "Marjorie, tomorrow on your way to school, say a man pulls up in a car and tells you he wants to take you to get some ice cream. What are you going to do?" Marjorie thought for a minute then responded, "Well, I guess I'm just going to have me a hot fudge Sunday!"
- One parent called me to tell her that her son had the mumps. I asked her how she knew that, and she responded. "he has a craving for pickles and that's a sure sign of mumps!" it's a good thing her only child was a boy!
- Another mother came by to brag that she had finally gotten rid of "it". I asked her what she meant by "it" and she said, "lice". When I asked her what she had done, she said simply, "I had the barber shave his head then I took him home and sprayed him with Raid."

- A 3rd grader had broken her arm falling from her 2nd story bedroom window because she "wanted to fly like Superman". When her dad asked her if she had learned a lesson, she replied, "Yup. Next time I'm going to wear my cape."
- That fall we had a 1st grader transfer. His first day during lunch he commandeered a chair and called 911 from the payphone in the hall. When the operator answered, he yelled, "Help I'm being held hostage!" she asked him where he was calling from and he said, "Woodruff School". The local police got a real kick out of that.
- One day I had to call home to talk to a dad. I started the conversation with, "Mr. Jones, I have good news and bad news for you. Remember Johnny's tooth that was loose when he left home? Well, the good news is it finally came out. The bad news is it was helped by Billy's fist".
- The next day we had to suspend a 4th grader because he would not quit cussing at the teacher. When his dad walked in to pick him up, the first words out of the dad's mouth were, "Gddm it, what the f… did you do now?" The next time we had to suspend George, to avoid more cussing my secretary told him to wait in the hall and, "yell when your Dad comes". Ten minutes later we head a bloodcurdling yell and cracked up. Humor was the constant that got us through the day.
- Two students were dealing with a mentally ill mother. I arranged a meeting with Social Services and list examples of her sickness: she sends them to school with only one shoe on, she locks the refrigerator when they're home, she hits them with hairbrushes, she sends them outside until it's so dark the street lights come on, etc. etc. etc. The social worker barely listens claiming "there's nothing" she can do even though I stress how dangerous and unbalanced the mother is and how vulnerable her kids are. Six weeks later her, 4th grade daughter, Ginny, dies of an overdose, and police can't decide whether it's suicide or homicide with the help of mom's pills.
- The 1st person Mom calls, of course, is me. When I go to the hospital, Mom runs to me and cries, "Help me. Help me." Her pleas make me want to vomit because I had been trying to help

her all year but now all I could do is hold Ginny's hand until the doctors declare her brain dead and unplug the machines. From then on, I had little respect for Protective Service personnel.

- Years later when I ran into her crazy mother, she made the comment, "Ginny had a long way to go and a short time to get there", then added, "if I'm stuck with kids, it should be up to me to decide how to handle them".
- In one of the strangest coincidences of my career, I met with a father on his lunch hour to go over some paperwork to get his son Special Ed services. He thanked me profusely and said, "In all the schools my son has ever attended (5 by that time), you are the only one to ever care enough about him to get him some help". I asked why so many schools he replied, "I was in prison for the past 7 years". When I asked what had sent him to prison, he said it was because he had been the boss of an auto smuggling ring. As he went over details from the past 10 years, it became clear he had stolen *my* car the first year I moved to town!
- Bennie Ray sounded out 3 words on a page and his teacher, Faye Metaj, excitedly asked, "Bennie Ray do you know what you're doing?" He says, defensively, "What? She replied, "You're reading!" And he leans back in his chair with a Cheshire grin and says, "I is?"
- One student, eager to get in early, banged on the door so hard he broke the window. I hesitated before making that home visit because I knew his older brother had just been arrested for arson. I was pleasantly surprised when his father suggested to have him work at school as a custodian every day until the window was paid for. He said, "I wish my older son (the arsonist) had had you as a principal; I think he would've learned a lot more respect for property".
- The second to the last day Stanley pushed another 6th grader into the chalkboard, and we had to call 911. All the way down the stairs I wrestled mentally with calling his father because, with 6 kids at our school, I was calling home frequently. I told myself, I wouldn't have to suspend Stanley because the next day was our farewell picnic and when he moved on to 7th grade, we'd never see him again. By the time I got to my office, my conscience had

> prevailed--I owed it to staff and our discipline code to follow through on suspension so I was relieved when no one answered the phone. Thirty minutes later, Stanley's dad stormed into the office, slammed the door, pointed his finger at me, and said, " I'll tell you one thing: this school district would be a hellva lot better off if every principal was as consistent as you!"

I knew then that our discipline plan was not only effective but highly respected by all of our stakeholders

At the end of my 4th year at Woodruff, I wasn't surprised when I got a visit from our new superintendent asking if I would agree to a voluntary transfer "to a school that has **real problems**" (Ironic, right?). He said he knew "there'd be a community uprising if it was involuntary" but he had to close Woodruff as it was the oldest and smallest school in the district and it would make more sense economically to send its students to two other schools nearby. If Woodruff stayed open, it would require extensive upgrading to make it code compliant. I knew that was accurate because we didn't even have a public address system due to faulty wiring. As much as I hated to admit it, I knew, too, what he said was true. Believing there is an art to knowing when to leave so I reluctantly said yes.

We had a farewell to end all farewells complete with a community pancake supper, fiddles, guitars and group singing and dancing. It was a bittersweet night I will always remember. The next day, as I packed up the many gifts and cards and cleared out my office, a Dione Warwick song, "I know I'll never love this way again…" kept running through my head because it was so apropos. I felt that my last day at Woodruff was the end of a colossal "love affair". I honestly thought I would never love "that way again"

Little did I know that there would be many more love affairs to come!

YOU SAW ME CRYING IN THE CHAPELLE

The next school, Chapelle, the one "**with real problems**", had a terrible climate and rampant staff dissension, mostly because of a principal who changed his mind every week. He was a tyrant who would sporadically make announcements that teachers could no longer send students to the office for discipline because he didn't have time to "bother" with them. He placed strips in the hallways to monitor traffic but rarely visited classrooms except to yell at someone for a perceived transgression. He would criticize staff in front of parents and did more paperwork than people work (it was rumored that he was working on his dissertation). His behavior and unpredictability caused many teachers to use excessive sick days just to get away from the tension in the building. Discipline was sporadic and inconsistent. Parents and students were confused about rules and consequences for deviant behavior. The entire school community hungered for clarity and fair consequences for all.

After meeting with staff members individually and then staff as a whole the first week to get input on what I could do to ease the tension, I decided to institute a weekly newsletter I named *Monday Briefs*.

It was obvious to me that part of the problem in the school was that staff never knew what to expect from one day to the next. This newsletter became a mechanism that lent predictability and routine as it outlined events planned such as assemblies or class field trips, basically anything that could affect teacher or student schedules. I highlighted staff accomplishments and accolades, when I would be visiting their classrooms, and district happenings. Agendas for staff meetings were posted well ahead of time and staff steering committees helped decide what topics would be on them. We created "Quality Circles" to garner and validate input from everyone, even the bus drivers and kitchen workers. This process is included under the heading of "Quality Circles Go to School" at the end of this book.

Using Title One monies I took the entire staff on a weekend spa retreat--complete with swimming, massages, games, and excellent catered meals to help us come together in a stress-free environment. Barriers began to come down as we started to gel. We started working together as a team, propping each other up when spirits drooped but, mostly, we started to have fun.

When the time seemed right, I shared blueprints for discipline that staff felt they could shape into a model that fit our students and circumstances at Chapelle. Tulani Smith helped champion the cause.

Interestingly, after just a few months of implementing our effective limit setting strategy at Chapelle, a 6th grader came up to me and said, "Boy, that discipline plan of yours is really working; we don't have any problems this year!" One of the teachers, Kay Brown, overheard him and said, "You're right, Bobby". This place used to be a rat race but now the cat is winning. With this pink slip, we've had nothing but peace!" Merrith Sayer's 1st grader came up to me and confided the next morning, "Mrs. Dignan, I told my mom about you guys" I asked her what she "told her". Kathy replied, "I told her how much you guys like me here cuz you're always correcting me!"

To make the community more involved with Chapelle, I instituted Take a Principal to Lunch weeks when I would bring a sandwich and an individual family—or group—would provide beverages and we'd discuss what was of most concern that particular month.

Every time we had a vacancy, I would solicit staff input while emphasizing our need to hire qualified minorities to reflect our community makeup more closely. Staff agreed, and these new hires went a long way in helping to earn the trust of both the kids and the community.

Since I had always been kid focused, I shared many of the activities and events that kids had enjoyed the most at Woodruff and encouraged staff to create some events Chapelle could call its own. We brainstormed a long time to come up with something we felt would involve and, better yet, include the community as a whole.

Thanks largely to our 5th grade teacher, Meg Lewandowski, we decided to create and pioneer an event we would name **Vehicle Day**.

Vehicle Day became the first of many exciting annual events and was featured in *Instructor Magazine*. Teachers devised week- long lesson plans that centered around jobs—especially those that had vehicles attached. English lessons would focus on trips, and the younger students traced cars and trucks for their writing journals. Math lessons would focus on the cost of gas, the ratio of miles per hour, load capacities, etc., while geography lessons would explore routes and places people with kids would want to go. I guess you could say by this time, we were "driven" to give Chapelle kids unique experiences.

Then came the day itself! On **Vehicle Day**, the parking lot was filled from 8 to late with everything from a helicopter to a hearse. We had cherry pickers, ambulances, race cars, horse and buggies, cookie trucks, piazza vans, Federal Express carriers, police cars and 18 wheelers—if it had wheels it was on display! Adding to the overall excitement were the squeals and laughs of kids getting in and out, honking horns, or mimicking driving a big truck or a fast car.

But probably the most significant part of the day involved the adults who had never had their jobs looked at through the eyes of an admiring child.

This, too, endeared us to parents who saw us ennobling career paths and professions other than doctor, lawyer, or proverbial Indian Chief.

When we added **Tool Day** to our roster the following year, parents were thrilled that we were acknowledging the importance of trade and crafts and blue-collar workers such as themselves.

On **Tool Day** we filled the gym and hallways with plumbers, hair/nail technicians, x ray technicians, carpenters, hardware displays, computer whizzes, weavers, chefs, and kilns. 43 occupations were represented in booths which kids visited to talk to the craftsmen and women or play with their tools.

Later that year, we initiated an ***International Luncheon*** where we invited all parents to bring in their favorite ethnic dish with a recipe and join us in native garb. We had 17 different nationalities represented and started a tradition that nourished all of us over the years.

The second year at Chapelle, I created a "Let's Be Good to Ourselves Day" with snacks and gifts I bought and placed in the lounge. To emphasize my appreciation for staff, I subbed in their rooms so teachers could get a

30 minute break to read the books or scarf down treats, or just plain relax. Throughout that year I would leave coupons in staff mail boxes to cash in with one day's notice saying things like, "I will take over your lunch duty" or "you can leave 30 minutes early today", or "why not come to work 30 minutes later tomorrow?", etc. By the 3rd year of my principalship at Chapelle, we were cited by Dr. Brookover, a national guru on school climate, **as having one of the best school climates in the country!**

At Chappelle we had other successes to celebrate as well, and many moments that were flat-out funny:

- One such occurred when our special ed teacher turned to open her door and the "knob" she grabbed by mistake belonged to the janitor.
- Our US Congressman had gifted us with a flag flown over the US Capitol. When the safety squad tried to fly it in a school-wide celebration, they hooked it to the chain upside down (which of course, was the picture on page one of the newspapers). One mortified 6th grader promising it wouldn't happen again, said, "Dr. Dignan, don't worry, we'll get the hang of it sooner or later".
- The same Congressman, the honorable Carl Pursell, put us in touch with Ludington Press, a prestigious book publishing company. When he accompanied the 80-year owner, Mr. Ludington, who wanted to donate 3000 books to our library, they overheard one of the 5th grade students complaining, "now I guess they'll expect us to start reading them!"
- The differences in cultures were evident in various ways—so much so that we hosted an Ethnic Lunch to highlight food and native costuming. At the event, a student from Italy said to the gym teacher, "Mr. Luplow, I seen you yesterday". I was walking by, so I corrected him by saying, "I SAW you yesterday" and he said, "You seen him, too?"
- Another time, Chinese parents came to the office to enroll their son and asked if I knew where they could learn English. When I told them they could get free lessons nightly at the high school, they jumped up joyfully in the air and I swear they clicked their

heels! I was reminded of an old Toyota commercial and wished all Americans were that grateful for a free education.

- Then there was the time at one of our staff meetings when our 5th grade teacher informed us that "the rabbit died", never noticing the teacher consultant turn pale because she thought he was referring to her secret pregnancy test instead of his room's pet.

And speaking of pregnancy, at the last staff meeting of the year I told the staff "I have something to share with you", and the 3rd grade teacher blurted out—as a joke—"you're pregnant" then fell off her chair laughing—until I told her she was right. The look on the faces in that room was priceless!

Of course, at that point in my life, (I guess to make sure I would never enjoy a dull moment--pregnant, successfully principalling, and working on my dissertation), the latest superintendent decided, once again, to transfer me to a school that had "**real problems**". This time the problems centered on social-economic disparities among families and dismal test scores for the entire school.

ARDIS

Fortunately, before I had become principal at Woodruff and Chapelle, I had created Parent Advisory Boards and administered Kindergarten Screening for the entire district. These positions helped me connect with diverse populations but, more importantly, taught me skills I could share with parents to increase special learning experiences, both at school and at home and included helping students with testing and homework. I also created a K.I.D.S. Program (Kindergarten Individualized Developmental Skills Program) to help dozens of kids succeed at young ages. This unique knowledge helped me set up parent workshops and counseling sessions for students who were not ready for kindergarten based on levels of maturation and readiness tests, and enabled me to gain credibility with Ardis families before school had even started that fall. It was my belief that failing students meant failing teachers, so I knew I had my work "cut out" for me in this assignment.

According to the state's measuring stick, only 45% of the students at Ardis were reading at grade level.

The student population was comprised of some of the richest families in the district, but many of the African American kids (38%) felt disenfranchised. Adding to the dichotomy, almost 50% of our students were eligible for free or reduced lunch.

In addition to the unique academic and economic disparities, 5 out of the district's 7 Board members had sons and daughters at Ardis, so politics went with the territory.

Adding to those challenges was the uniqueness of the building itself.

Ardis had been constructed as an "open school". That meant rooms had no walls, so noise, traffic, and chaos were omnipresent within the center that bordered every space available.

And once again, staff ruled.

Teachers thought they would still be able to run the school and I would be a pushover because I was (very) pregnant…" And everyone knows pregnant women miss a lot of work". (Despite the fact that, when I gave birth to my daughter on a Friday night ten years previously, I returned to work the following Monday! At that time—April 21, 1972—maternity leave did not exist, so, even though I had 30 sick days, I was not allowed to use them. The law changed 2 months later).

Traditionally, Ardis teachers had been able to choose which basal series and book companies they wanted to use, not realizing that the mere act of promoting students every year from one grade to the next brought new vocabulary demands. And, because one of the things staff felt proudest of was their "independence", they felt either insulted or threatened when I told them use of different series between grades contributed to our low student achievement and dismal test scores.

Meanwhile, complaints about black students not being challenged or fairly treated had been festering for a long time, so I met with angry parents my first month to assure them they, also, had a voice.

That night after the meeting, I went into labor and gave birth prematurely. Jimmy was born severely handicapped, he had no eyes, a true mid-line cleft palate (only the 3rd the nation's expert at U of M had ever seen) and, literally, only half a brain. Because he was 6 weeks premature and needed to stay in an incubator with parades of doctors arguing over his condition, I spent nights in his room then returned to work fulltime two weeks later.

Although Jimmy was considered a "failure to thrive baby" and had to be tube-fed, he confounded doctors by tripling his birthweight when he came home before dying of pneumonia 5 months later. Blind, deaf, and crippled according to doctors, Jimmy had only a sense of touch, so we held him 24/7. John,12, and Cassandra,10, loved him dearly and would often take him to play with their friends or feed and rock him at night. As Cassandra said upon hearing of all his handicaps, "that's okay we'll take him anyway he comes!"

Patrick and I could not have been prouder of our kids for the way they embraced their little brother and, when our priest asked if we would let Jimmy represent baby Jesus at the children's Christmas Mass, they piped up, "only if we get to hold him." So that year they were Mary and Joseph and there wasn't a dry eye in the church.

The families and staff joined in the love fest for our little one as well, encouraged by Cindy Hackney and Benni Hebrew, parents and teachers began taking turns bringing dinner every night while Jimmy was in the hospital, offering to help with transportation or errands while we took care of him. Though only in our lives a short while, Jimmy brought the school community home to us. We were loved!

Staff members were compassionate and became much more supportive because it was clear that I had not only placed my son and family at the top of my priorities, but I still worked hard at school and remained committed to making Ardis even better.

Surprisingly, they agreed when I suggested hiring a national textbook consultant to build consensus on a single series. Furthermore, they enthusiastically rolled up their sleeves and helped analyze skill sets required by our state testing program (MEAP) through a backward engineering process I taught them.

This process was not only arduous but, ultimately, extremely rewarding as proven by our new scores.

We developed a system that was not only collaborative but produced visible results. Each grade level teacher would write lesson plans focusing on a specific skill for a week. (For example, one 1st grade teacher would devise a plan working on homonym/synonyms to share with all the other 1st grade teachers; thus, teachers only had to worry about writing lesson plans for their grade every 3 weeks).

In addition, any "down" time, like 5-10 minutes before gym, lunch, or recess, was to be used to drill kids on that day's particular skill. And we creatively included parents in our school-wide strategy. I wrote a weekly newsletter emphasizing which skills we were working on each week, asking them to find examples (e.g. synonyms/homonyms, opposites/similarities, etc.) in their interactions with their kids.

The results of our collaborative efforts were remarkable**: 86% of our students** were ranked as proficient in the state-wide testing program that year—as contrasted with only 45% the year I arrived! Ardis was recognized by that 2nd year as **1 of the top 20 schools in the state of Michigan** for improved test scores!

At Ardis, we were also extremely fortunate to have a dynamo heading our PTO; I swear Bea Kuwik bled school colors, doing absolutely everything she could to connect parents and teachers which helped our students flourish. Whether it was a School Carnival (where I got dunked repeatedly in the water tank) or a school-wide fundraiser, under Bea's tutelage, we made over $33,000 one year for computers and the following year enough to build an entirely new playground! That's a lot of candy bars to get high on!

We decided it was a good time to teach kids how to "get high" on things beside sugar (or drugs) by doing something that involved both mind and body and would be unique to Ardis. We named the seminal undertaking a **Fair of Natural Highs** and it was fantastic! Thanks to Jovita Davis and Marilyn Bishop, we electrified the student body, the staff and the community with a day-long extravaganza that included calligraphy and cheerleading, dog grooming, art, drama, piazza making and cartooning; by the time I left as its principal, Ardis had as many as 25 offerings to involve kids and families. The final year I was there we featured a **Renaissance Fair,** complete with a marketplace and old-world costuming.

Ardis became a great school. While Bea continued her magic on parents, staff worked well together, and we continued to impact student achievement dramatically.

The only thorn in my side was my new boss.

In his 1st year in Ypsilanti, he upset people by hiring his wife as a school nurse so she could (apparently) use our sick bank to have her hip replaced on the school's dime. That was bad enough, but he wanted to assign her to my school, and I refused. I told him we had too many chronically ill kids who had been seeing the same nurse for 3 years and I would not consider disrupting those relationships. He never forgave me and did everything he could to undermine me from that point on.

First, he made me take a new 1st grade teacher—a friend's daughter who had only taught adult ed and, thus, was not suited for 1st grade—then he would thwart any new vacancy at Ardis by stalling decisions. Shockingly, not only did he give that 1st grade teacher his own private number so she would have him on speed dial whenever she wanted to lodge a complaint about me but, at the end of the year, HE ACTUALLY CHANGED HER EVALUATION which was against the law. When

I complained to the state organization, he insisted that we go before an ad hoc committee comprised of people he chose and consuming over 30 hours of presentation of "evidence" of my "bias". Surprisingly, his hand-picked committee determined that my ratings were fair and should stand as written.

It became increasingly clear that he and I were in a situation I could neither tolerate nor change. I knew there would be a power struggle between us as long as we were in the same district. Although I had been in the Ypsilanti School District for 20 years and it didn't seem fair that I was the one who would have to sacrifice moving from a place that had meant so much to me, I decided I had to go.

As I told my students at Eastern in the administration classes I taught, there is an art to knowing when to leave. Whenever a conflict arises between a superintendent and a principal, the superintendent will prevail.

Knowing I could no longer work for someone whom I did not respect, I had lunch the next day with a friend who encouraged me to apply for an Assistant Superintendent position in Milan, only 14 miles away.

I applied immediately and surprised even myself by getting it.

As fate would have it, the superintendent who hired me as his assistant, said that my former boss badmouthed me in superintendent meetings all the time, so he knew if "that man" didn't like me, I must be doing something right!

Although I started under contract with Milan Area Schools 2 months later, I made it part of our agreement that I could take off as much time as I needed that summer because my mother was dying and I wanted to help care for her. Whenever my mother slept from her doses of morphine, I wrote grants or read over district paperwork to gain a necessary and quick appreciation of the past history and current issues facing my new district.

My mother died Labor Day weekend, so I started the year when the rest of the staff did.

Milan ended up being the best thing that could ever have happened to me. Especially in my grief.

There was not a day that went by that someone didn't stop in my doorway to thank me for some task I had just performed or some meeting that impacted the direction of the schools in the district. Staffs at Milan had been waiting for what they called "a breath of fresh air" to address issues that had been on the back burner for quite a while. The superintendent had been there almost 30 years so change was not happening soon enough for many who were looking for more cohesive curriculum and policies.

Because it was a small district, my responsibilities covered every aspect of it. I was put in charge of busing, staffing—both hiring and firing—and operations and grounds. Furthermore, we had to rely on bond issues to keep us afloat; I was responsible for running millage campaigns and was successful having all 5 of them pass over the next 7 years. In fact, when I determined I was ready to leave 8 years later, I told the Board I would not go until we passed a bond issue for a new high school which we did on the first try.

I became adept—almost psychic—at hiring new staff. I would think to myself we really need a new physical ed teacher who also has a strong math background (an unusual combination), and the next day an application with just that combination would end up on my desk. What I was proudest of though, is that I hired the first African American administrator in the district and then kept finding minorities to fill slots as they became vacant. The assistant principal from Detroit would joke that every time he passed my office he felt like he should 'genuflect' because I had hired him to work in such a great place.

I worked on grants to supplement our small district's funding and was gratified to win an $80,000 grant from the state of Michigan for drug-free schools. This grant helped galvanize prestigious business leaders to join my District Wide Advisory Board and work directly with kids and staffs to help students find other alternatives and take strong stands against drugs. I had named the initiative EMPOWER and that is exactly what it did. We even set up a Teen Center (see appendix). In addition to the grant helping kids, I brought PRIDE to the district which was a program out of Atlanta that taught parents how to raise drug-free kids. My Milan parents were so impressed with the training (led by who else? Bea Kuwik and another respected, energetic Ypsilanti parent, Eddie Kosky) that we decided to offer it to surrounding school districts. By the end of its first year, PRIDE had impacted over 200 parents!

We streamlined curriculum in all the major subject area to make our offerings relevant and aligned with emerging state standards. By working closely with the agricultural teacher to bring animals and equipment to school grounds for elementary students, we created **Ag Day**, which became an annual event showcasing Future Farmers of America students. Pictures are included in the Appendix.

Milan was an exceptional place to work. The teachers were as eager to learn new skills as the students. The administrators worked cohesively together and were open to trying anything that involved kids. Community pride and involvement were among the highest I had ever seen.

Sports, too, were important. We were the Milan Big Reds and to play on our teams was considered special; so special that my involvement in two cases led me to a law degree.

The first case involved a junior at the high school. One of his teachers had just found out that he had molested his (the teacher's) pre-school daughter when he babysat her while in middle school. Because the girl did not have the requisite maturity or vocabulary to describe the acts at the time, she had not told her parents until she turned 9. The student was chastised by the juvenile court when these actions came to light but, other than being on probation for a year, had no other consequences.

Unfortunately, the student was now not only in the aggrieved father's class but also played defense on the varsity team which the father coached. Knowing the court had already done as much as it deemed appropriate 4 years later, the student would provoke the teacher by blocking his path, making comments under his breath, and subtly dare him to do anything about it. One night when the teacher and his wife were in a local restaurant, the student sauntered in and Dad blew up, yelled expletives and "rapist" to the chagrin of the other patrons.

On Monday morning the teacher came to my office to confess and asked if I could do anything about this untenable situation. I informed him that—because it occurred off school grounds and, on a weekend, there was nothing I could do—unless the parents asked me to intervene.

Well, sure enough, they made an appointment that day to report the teacher's "terrible and embarrassing behavior" and asked me to do "something to punish" him. I promised that I would investigate the situation for both sides and get back to them promptly because football was starting.

I spent 56 hours interviewing anyone who had observed either the teacher or the student so I could formulate a fair and reasonable decision.

The teacher's union became involved as did friends of the family. The union threatened that if I did anything to sanction the teacher, they would grieve all the way up to the state level. But I paid special attention to the football staff's opinions because it was on the field and in the locker rooms, on the bus and in the weight room that intimacy and tension between both parties would be exacerbated and observed by the rest of the players.

I also did research on constitutional rights of players and found that there was no fundamental requirement for students to play sports. My investigation was thorough, even questioning the high school athletic association and 7 other coaches—including my husband (without providing names). After a thorough and painstaking process, I concluded that Dad should not have to be demoted to the junior varsity with reduced pay just to avoid daily confrontation with this student. After talking to the head varsity coach and discovering that this junior would be sitting on the bench the next 2 seasons anyway due to upcoming defensive players who were bigger and faster, I decided to allow the student to play on the ***junior varsity t***eam, thus avoiding any more clashes between the two. I must admit I thought my solution was brilliant even though I knew the student and his family would not agree. In a closed session I presented my rationale to the Board of Education the following night.

The family had come to the meeting well prepared, accompanied by the head of the lawyer's association and a nationally recognized juvenile mental health expert who both argued at length about the damage this would do to a young man, "whose future depended on football and, if denied that outlet, might become suicidal…." I simply sat and took notes then demolished their arguments with the results of my investigation. The Board unanimously echoed my recommendation then, on the way to the parking lot, asked if I had ever considered a career in law. That planted the seed, but it wasn't until the following year that it was given fertilizer.

And all because "we had to give a hoot" about another Milan Red Skin challenge.

Ray Hoot was a sophomore who dropped into my office one day and asked why he couldn't ride the bus to accompany his baseball team to Adrian. After checking into it, I found Ray hadn't maintained the requisite grade point average to play on the team that week. Over the next few months, Ray visited me often so I could help him with the subjects he found most difficult. Because he was flunking, it was determined that he would have to attend summer school if he hoped to be on the football team that fall. The problem for Ray was that the closet summer school program was in Ypsilanti, two blocks from our house. I checked with my husband and kids, both of whom were close to Ray's age, and asked what they thought about having him live with us that summer. Ray would have been the 5th student for whom we had provided a temporary home by then, so I wasn't surprised when they all agreed. An added bonus was the fact that my husband was considered "the Dean of Baseball" in the area and our son, John, was being scouted heavily by baseball coaches and organizations. His parents couldn't believe we would go the extra mile for their son and were thrilled that—as educators, we would naturally see to his academic skill sets as well.

That summer Ray improved in baseball, football, and academics, often sitting with us when we came home from work to go over his assigned vocabulary, reading and spelling materials and would positively glow when he got everything right. The second week with us, his mother was hospitalized with a heart attack and when I went to see her, she made me promise "if anything happens" we'd watch out for Ray.

When Ray returned to school that fall, Milan teachers could not believe it was the same kid; the first semester he blew them away by making the honor roll. But then, Ray being Ray, he started to slip and within 3 months he was beginning to fail and would not be eligible to play baseball.

His parents found a doctor to diagnose him as having hyperactive attention deficit disorder and sued the school district for not recognizing his "handicap". The lawsuit shocked the school community but moved ahead full steam. Because of the costs associated with defending such a claim both in terms of time and money, I recommended we settle but with a caveat—no money was to go to the family. We crafted a remedy that required Ray to keep going to school after he graduated to claim it. We agreed that $5000 would be paid directly to a community college of his choice for books, tuition, and lab fees; if attendance was not satisfactory, he would lose it all. The community considered this a great win for us; so did we!

Previously, I had kept the district out of court 5 times so it was becoming obvious to me that if I wanted to someday be successful as a superintendent, I would need to learn more about school law. I enrolled in Detroit College of Law that week, thus beginning a nightly 100-mile trek to earn my second doctorate.

Now I could get back to my ***real job***: improving education and discipline throughout the system. We had offered adult education to the forensic center staff as well as to the federal prison for years; in fact, our adult ed program generated a large part of our district revenue. I was asked to give the graduation speech that year and lost sleep over it! What do you say to a prison population about graduating? Education will make you free? You have now broadened your horizons? I finally settled on the theme, "Are you serving time or is time serving you? It was a big hit and I took the message to heart because I knew time had to start serving me now that I was commuting to law school in addition to my ongoing responsibilities both at work and at home. Luckily, my husband pitched in on housework so I could either be a student or a superintendent every weekend for the next two years.

It was during those years that millages and bond issues were constants eating up even more time and attention. The Superintendent had decided I should handle all millages and bond issues from that point forward. As a rural farming community, Milan's frequent but necessary attempts to tax land for more money was always fraught with challenge. To help convince taxpayers of our needs, we created community groups and individuals who would help us get the message our through letters to the editor, coffee klatches, public appearances and even placemats in all the local restaurants. We succeeded every time due to these laborious and transparent strategies. (See samples in Appendix)

But the state had other ideas. The following year they passed a bill that put us in receivership due to lack of our usual funding. It was at this time the superintendent decided to retire and kept the dreadful fiscal news from the teachers and the community at large. Whenever I'd see him manipulate the budget he would present to the board, I would question him on his creative math and his response was consistent, "But the Board doesn't want to see negatives". I told him 'but, Clayt, they have to know about the negatives whether they want to or not". I believe that seeing the district's fiscal future becoming a picture of doom and gloom led to his decision to retire.! As a result of closely guarding his "creative budgeting", when I succeeded him as superintendent months later, the entire district thought I was to blame for the mess. Even my daughter, Cassandra, who was doing her student teaching at Paddock at the time, pleaded with me to let staff know the truth about the deficit; I refused, telling her Clayt had served the district well for 40 years and since he still lived in Milan, I would protect him from the fallout even if that meant I got the blame. Which, of course, I did.

Michigan had given us 3 years to fix the inherited deficit, but I brought us out of receivership the 1st year by scrutinizing every program, person, and function we were underwriting and paying close attention. Due to my fierce examination of every class roster and program, only one student's schedule was impacted!

The Superintendency in Milan was a lifelong dream and I would probably still be there today if it had not been for the retirement quirks in Michigan's pension system. Actuarial studies had shown that after contributing to the system 31 years, the law of diminishing returns kicked in and every year after the 31st projected—over time—a corresponding loss in benefits. I was getting close to that marker so, once again, I knew it was time to leave. But I had one job left to do.

I had promised the Board that I would not leave Milan until we passed a huge bond issue to build a new high school. It was successful the 1st time despite naysayers—including my business manager—saying it would never pass!

That month I applied for out-of-state superintendencies.

Before I had come to Milan, discrimination against female superintendents was the norm. I have included some references in the Addendum: for example, one school system, Willow Run, considered me as one of their two finalists but, according to one of the Board members, "we would take a Persian Jew before we'd risk hiring a female superintendent" which is what they did!

The second district I had applied to, Manchester, was a conservative farming community and backward when it came to hiring a woman. Although I was once again one of two finalists. When the Board visited my school, they asked me such questions as, "if you were walking toward a door the same time as a man was walking through a door, would you let him open it for you? " or "if you got this job, would your husband move, too?"

These were the kinds of questions I was subjected to while being vetted for a superintendent's position. Can you imagine asking this of a man?

But to make matters even worse, during the final Board meeting to determine its new Superintendent, Manchester Board members stated such things as, "Dr Dignan is more competent, more intelligent, more experienced, more innovative and more knowledgeable about school reform but she's a woman, so we'll go with our number two choice..." They stated all of this **in public!** I could have sued them but felt they—at least—were honest about their rationale. Besides I had learned from my mentor during my PEP days that, if I wanted a successful career in the county, I had to avoid lawsuits about discrimination. In 1970, When the Ypsilanti Board had given Ken a 14% raise the second year of PEP and me none, even though we were equals and, according to our boss, Pete Kingston, "we think you're head and shoulders above Ken but you're pregnant now and if the baby gets sick, you'll stay home whereas if Ken's kids get sick, his wife will stay home". When I said, "but, Pete, that's illegal and flagrant discrimination", he replied "I know and I would go to court to help you fight, but remember if you sue schools over sex discrimination, you'll get a reputation as a feminist and no one else will ever hire you in this county". Pete died of cancer 2 months later and any idea of going to court died with him. But I knew it was sound advice.

After telling Milan's Board of Education that I would begin to find out-of-state positions, I became a finalist for Superintendent in 6 states but, **almost 30 years later**, being a female was still considered a detriment!

I have added tips on **How to Break Through the Glass Ceiling without Having to Sweep Up the Mess** at the end of this narrative based on my many experiences of being the "first" female in many categories, e.g. 1st woman Community School Director in the country, one of the 1st women head-start directors under JFK, 1st female principal in the 70s in Ypsilanti, 1st (and only female) President of Ypsilanti Principal's Association, 1st female Superintendent in Monroe County, and 1st female Superintendent in the greater Washington, D.C, area.

Thus, ends a 30-year career in Michigan and the beginnings of my next journey into the roiling rivers of leadership where I learned that you can never enter a river at the same spot and once you leave its flow, your footsteps are erased forever.

APPENDIX

PEP: Personalized Educational Program
Project PEP was the first middle/high school alternative Ed program in the country

How to Break Through the Glass Ceiling without Having to Sweep Up the Mess
Subtle and blatant sex discrimination affected my 50-year career and continues today

Quality Circles Go to School
A construct for getting more dynamic and productive staff involvement throughout the school

Discipline that Works
A strategic approach to helping students internalize control and teachers maintaining their sanity

PROJECT PEP: a personalized educational program for an alternative junior and senior high school

In 1968, at the request of Ypsilanti administrators, Ken Burnley and I started an alternative middle/high school for dropouts and troubled youth who kept getting kicked out of their traditional schools. PEP was the first program of its kind in the state of Michigan and was domiciled in an old house by the tracks. Students who had been suspended or considered "hopeless' were transferred to our little building throughout the year with no concern about typical semesters.

The school demographics today would have been shocking to most administrators in the late 60s and early 70s but, ironically, many of today's children are more akin to that student population in 1968 than their own counterparts. More than half of our population at PEP were minorities, many at the poverty level, and from single family homes due to illegitimacy, death, divorce, or desertion. Our students had noticeably short attention spans even without a ubiquitous cell phone.

The only advantage our PEP kids had over today's student was, usually, a mother in the home before, during, and after school. Today's students often come home to an empty house, missing not only the comfort and consistency a built-in mother provides, but also a curriculum "hidden" and taken for granted: learning to count, to say ABCs, to recite nursery rhymes and to hold conversations with an adult or other family member. Many disenfranchised youth have no one in their corner to cheer them on from the time they take their first steps to reading their first word; even more discouraging, many of today's troubled students have no one to hold their hands over the inevitable bumps of adolescence.

To say we witnessed the inevitable "bumps of adolescence" was an understatement. We actually had the most violent students in the district—I remember during the first month facing a gun, 4 knives, and a hatchet all in the same day!

Not only was our student body unique but so was our schedule and our curriculum. We only had kids half days that first year so we could meet with their families, case workers and other agencies and create a curriculum that would keep them in school. We told kids we would explore all possible avenues in their future and would help them excel at them. If they wanted to become a doctor, we would help; if they wanted to join the armed forces, we'd make it possible, if their choices leaned toward a life of crime and public assistance, we would help them acquire the necessary skills for that path as well. We also started out with no rules—kids could skip school with no consequences, they could smoke all over the house without reprisal, they could play pool all day long in the lounge if they so desired. Obviously, we were winging it.

In the 3rd week Ken and I met to set up some basic rules but were pleasantly surprised when a group of kids interrupted our meeting to ask if they could see us in private. They said they felt that having no rules added to the stress and frequent fighting. They cited examples of "certain kids" always hogging the pool table and said that even the kids who didn't smoke felt compelled to try it. They asked if we would let them set up rules around attendance, smoking, and better use of their time. Of course, we agreed wholeheartedly.

The difference was astounding! Kids—not teachers—corrected kids.

Staff around the district could not believe these were the same kids they had feared so much they felt they had to send them away.

But, perhaps the most amusing phenomenon that occurred was the fact that—if we were late—the kids *broke into the house* to be counted as present—these were the same kids who had been charged with breaking and entering homes but never schools; in fact, they were more apt to break out of school by skipping or getting suspended! Our attendance averaged 96% for the rest of the year.

Another phenomenon that made colleagues jealous: police thought our kids belonged to a club because they never had to deal with them anymore—if they saw them throughout the day to ask why they weren't in school, our kids would answer proudly, "But we are. We're in PEP!"

On April 23, 1971, Judge O'Brien from Washtenaw County Juvenile Court chided Ann Arbor for not having "such a remarkable program to keep kids off the streets and in school... We think PEP's existence has saved the county money by reducing the number of institutional placements. As an educated guess, at least 12 of the kids on their list would have been placed in juvenile detention without the help of this fine program. Average cost of placement $5000 per year/per child = $60,000 a year..."

The second year, when I became pregnant with my 1st child, Ken asked me not to return after I gave birth, because my replacement "would have a hard enough time trying to earn the kids' trust and would never get them on her side if they thought there was any chance" I was coming back.

I knew he was right, so the district hired me as a Parent Consultant through Title I to create Parent Advisory Boards, make home visits to the disenfranchised, work on the upcoming district-wide census, and administer Kindergarten Screening.

But we had learned a lot of lessons from the kids at PEP. Perhaps the most important one was the constant reminder that *parents are still sending us the best kids they have.* In some respects, today's kids start out smarter and more conditioned to mental and visual stimulation. But they also tune out more quickly when things get "boring", or a task requires more time than just microwaving popcorn. The secret to success with PEP students remains the secret for **all** school success: Meet kids where they are and take them to greater heights!

Today's principals are in a unique position to do just that. Not only can they hire teachers who "turn kids on", they can weed out the ones who are turning them off. They can be instrumental in connecting homes with classrooms and classrooms with the "real world". They can create their own schoolwide events and keep kids coming back for more. This book alludes to just a few examples, but whether it's Vehicle Day or a Health Fair, there are ways to make kids want to come to school for more than just socialization and to get away from a bad home life.

But before learning the "hows" of running their schools, principals must be aware of the "whys". Principals eager to bring dramatic and even not-so-dramatic changes to their buildings must first realize that *the single most important element in any effective school is the level of expectation* for students and staff. Chapters in this book will show how to systematically raise the levels of expectation high enough to have a measurable impact on student achievement. Establishing high expectations is one of the most critical things a principal can do to bring improvement. A plan also saves principals from looking indecisive and from parents saying they're inconsistent or unfair.

I want to underscore that it's not the knock-down, drag-out fights that burn both principals and teachers out (the discipline strategies outlined in this book take care of those *very* effectively), but, rather, the "garbage behaviors" we have to put up with in today's public school environments: rampant lack of respect from students and parents, bickering, bullying, name-calling, tattling, talking back, the "I forgot my homework", or walking away while a teacher is talking, the poor attitudes and behaviors that make teaching exhausting and principaling inconsistent. Without a building-wide plan, schools drive some of our best teachers out of education and the worst ones to more deviance and discouragement. Principals would do well to remember, it is not the mountain ahead that tires us out, it's the pebbles of sand in our shoe. Principals must love what they're doing and maintain a sense of humor.

Their job is not unlike *Mission Impossible*; the only difference is that *everything* self-destructs, especially principals, if they can't inspire teachers to care for the very kids who challenge them the most.

HOW TO BREAK THROUGH THE GLASS CEILING WITHOUT HAVING TO SWEEP UP THE MESS

It used to be that females in administration were a little like old AVIS ads. They often started out in the number 2 spot but if/when they finally made it to the top, it was because they had to try harder, work longer, and make fewer mistakes along the way.

I was the first female Community School Director in the country. I was one of JFK's first female Head Start Directors in California. I was the first (and youngest) female County Administrator in Washtenaw County; the first female principal in the 1970s in Ypsilanti, the first female Superintendent in Monroe County in 1992, and the first female Superintendent in the greater Washington D. C. area in 1995. I "broke" many ceilings along the way. I also avoided stepping in the glass by recognizing these rules necessary to survive in a male world:

1. Female administrators who come on like gangbusters can intimidate or "turn off" males while confusing females by forgetting what got them into administration in the 1st place: people skills.
2. Subordinates allow fewer missteps from a female boss. The most mixed message I ever received in my 50 years of administration came from seven women who complained to my superior that I was "too calm and positive" during a crisis. Fortunately, even he saw the contradiction in that.

3. I even had a female teacher once tell me that she thought I was an exceptional leader because "we can't even tell when you're having your period!". It is best to let comments like that slide.
4. One of the major mistakes new female administrators make occurs when they unnecessarily flex muscles of power instead of realizing, by virtue of their position, they are already powerful—they are the boss.
5. Less-confident female principals err by frequently reminding others that they are women. Comments such as, "You're just saying that because I'm a woman" irritate and antagonize everyone—male and female alike.
6. Women need to avoid imitating men; saying something "pisses" them off; adopting "male" language, does nothing to raise a female's stature in the eyes of their counterparts.
7. Women need to be armed with a sense of humor instead of thin skin. In this book, I referred earlier to being the only female out of 28 administrators and, 3 years later, being unanimously chosen as the President of their Administrator's Union. I believe that elevating me to their President had to do with respect I had garnered from the men by just being myself, and not being easily intimidated. For example, our union meetings were always held in a bar and at my first meeting I sat next to a bruiser who liked to throw his weight around. It was summer, so we were all dressed casually, me in shorts and a top with a big zipper down the middle. Harold learned over and said, "I wonder what would happen if I pulled this zipper down?" Without missing a beat, I said, "Go ahead and try it…you'll find out why everyone calls you Smash Thumb!" The 27 other men roared! And, just like that, I was in. (incidentally, that was what everyone called him because he was a shop teacher and forever getting banged up).
8. In early effective school research, Brookover and Lezotte suggested the importance of delegating tasks and having faith in the competence of others. While all administrators have to give up some reins to help other people grow, *women are so used to doing so many things* for themselves this can sometimes be one of the most difficult adjustments for them to make when moving up.

9. Anthony Jay warned in *Management and Machiavelli*, that original "skill sets" can become barriers to advancement. Again, in this regard, women are often disadvantaged since teaching is usually the skill they have worked on the longest. But if people only see their leader as "a consummate teacher", it becomes difficult to for them to see her as anything else.
10. Jay also cautions that the more credit and goodwill one gets from "below", the less one gets "from above". Because personal loyalties are downward, "first to your own ideas then to the people who can help you realize them", it is imperative for women to win opposition over to neutrality rather than create a private army.
11. Women need to be especially on the alert for flattery. It is essential for them to hunt for disquieting advice and not be distracted by complements
12. Women must follow their intuition (what men call their "guts") when making the really difficult decisions, and listen to what people **aren't** saying.
13. In the *Art of Being the Boss*, Schoenberg describes a good administrator as one who has a universal desire to succeed. Such a person is aggressive, dependable, exhibits good judgment, a sense of urgency, and high expectations. Being a good administrator requires vision, thick skin, and sometimes a big mouth--which is all right if you're male—but, unfortunately, have to be toned down if you're female.
14. Both male and female leaders must do their homework, often weighing pros and cons that carry big risks. But, women need to remember in all matters, "to thy own self be true".
15. Women should gratefully allow men to promote them within the organization. I had a principal who wanted me to become his Community School Director (which meant I would become the first female in the country to do so), when he met with resistance from central office, he held out two documents and said, "here's my recommendation and here's my resignation…take your pick". Needless to say, I got the job.
16. Anthony Jay insists that a successful leader seeks criticism but cannot succeed without confidence or doubt, as "confidence is

essential for group morale, while self-doubt keeps us sensitive to our own errors". Women need to be especially apt at balancing the two,

17. Women who are "control freaks" sometimes delegate reluctantly then tie their subordinates *down* to specific processes, forgetting that once they tie people down to doing things "their way", *they bind themselves up* making sure their decisions are carried out.
18. Female administrators must allow for others be creative; in the end this improves the process *and* the final product. It is a female's primary responsibility to help people grow.
19. A crucial piece of advice for female administrators deals with belittling others. Never be the originator or conveyor of gossip. Always listen to yourself as though someone overhearing you will distort things. Because they will. If someone says, "so and so did me wrong", one technique defusing situations is to say, "That's funny, because she always says the nicest things about you"
20. Praise your employees to each other; a compliment that comes through a third person is even better than getting it firsthand.
21. But, most of all, treat everyone with respect. Use your intelligence, your intuition, and heightened sensitivity to understand and appreciate others. The "most important message above all" is others is to expect the best and the rest will come.

QUALITY CIRCLES GO TO SCHOOL

Improving School Climate through Student, Staff, and Community Involvement

In addition to instructional issues, several trends have noted that *school climate, organizational culture*, and *decision-making practices* have profound impact on student learning. These trends emphasize implications of research which indicate that appropriate participation and "involvement" at all levels of a school district correlate with many measures of effective learning. Researchers such as Brookover, Kyle, Lazotte, Thompson, Purkey & Smith tell us **what**'s important in school involvement but not **how** it's done. This brief paper highlights a process that markedly improves school climate and involves all stakeholders.

Schools have traditionally emphasized "top-down" and "chain-of command" procedures for information gathering, problem solving, implementation, and final aspects of any decision-making process. As a result, many attempts at "bottom-up" involvement have floundered often enough that participants have become frustrated and angry, or just plain bewildered by a mass of confusing and sometimes contradictory expectations, directives and norms.

School buildings are like small communities—desiring improvement but highly resistant to temporary disruptions of culture and custom which are required when innovation is introduced. Thus, with few tested, replicable procedures for school or district-wide participatory approaches to problem solving, many schools end up curtailing, faking, or finally, abandoning the whole idea.

While schools were concentrating on other issues, businesses were perfecting "Quality Work Circles" and developing parallel structures whose norms were systematic and compatible with pyramidal hierarchies. The widely accepted components require some adaptation from the Deming and Japanese management methods when applied to schools. In translating the QWL model to school systems, where the identifiable "products" are test scores, the logical Quality Circle is found in the classroom with the teacher functioning as *supervisor* and the students forming the problem-solving *work crew.*

Training sessions are held to teach concepts and skills to identify classroom-based problems and opportunities, engage in appropriate fact-finding, set goals, brainstorm alternative solutions, discuss likely consequences, develop action plans, test and implement plans, evaluate results and, ultimately, "fine tune" their plans as a result of those evaluations. Students learn that complex issues require commitment and patience since a single action plan usually takes several days before a plan is put into action. The classroom solving unit is called a Pupil Involvement Circle (PI Circle) and any building can support as many PI Circles as there are classrooms. These PI Circles are encouraged to meet daily, for 15 minutes at a time.

Many school districts have attempted to institutionalize similar kinds of participation at the staff level by creating "building leadership teams" or "principal advisory committees" and other structures expected to develop decision-making procedures among teaching staffs and their principals. Unfortunately, these problem-solving groups rarely live up to their potential but teachers who discover the benefits of interacting systematically with Pupil Involvement Circles in their classroom are quick to suggest that staff/administrator interactions might profit from similar procedures.

What seems to work best is a group of professional staff meeting twice a month with the building administrator as a Staff Involvement Group (SI Group) which follows predicable guidelines consistent with QWL concepts:

1. The building administrator (and building rep if there is a union) are present at all meetings.
2. All other participation is voluntary SI participants are committed to participate for the remainder of the school year and the first 3 meetings of the fall semester

3. The meeting manager (facilitator) is a member of the building's team, trained to lead the interactive group meetings (building administrator and union rep do not facilitate Meetings)
4. All meetings are open, and any staff member may join.
5. Outside resources may join temporarily where this is appropriate.
6. Group recommendations are reached by *consensus*; and the building administrator retains *responsibility* for all decisions. Since the building administrator is a participant and since all recommendations require consensus, all the groups final recommendations are implemented.
7. Only building-level issues are discussed.
8. Agendas and working papers are posted for total staff viewing.
9. Brief minutes are kept for each meeting.
10. Group produces *recommendations* and the administrator retains *responsibility* for all *decisions.*
11. There is an established, predictable time sequence and procedure for administrator to accept or reject the SI Groups recommendation.
12. All stakeholders are given opportunities for input at various stages of problem-solving
13. An effective range of communication channels are established and maintained.
14. Individual and temporary task forces are formed, monitored, and supported by the Si Group when complex problems require extra time and commitment
15. Building level Involvement Groups are composed of individuals with *homogenous* roles. Different SI Groups may be formed for a variety at the building level: a Teacher Involvement Group (TI) a Pupil Personal Involvement Group (PPI), a Lunchroom Supervisor's Group (LSI and a Family Involvement Group (FI) are a few examples.
16. All groups must be trained. And Minutes are sent to Central Office to keep them in the loop.

Further detailed procedures and research sources can be acquired by contacting the author at pygmalionprincipal@netzero.net

DISCIPLINE THAT WORKS

Helping Students Internalize Control

While the term "discipline" can be used in a variety of ways, educators agree that an effective disciplinary system is one that is consistently clear, producing predictable consequences while emphasizing intrinsic and extrinsic controls. Such a system acknowledges authoritarian control, self-control, peer control, and environmental controls where appropriate, but it also stresses student responsibility for deviant behavior.

The theory, principles and concepts underlying this approach were first described in a program developed for individual children by Smith and Smith (Smith & Smith, Judith &Donald, Child Management: A Program for Parents and Teachers, Champaign Illinois: Research Press, 1976) and later espoused by Glasser, Morse and others, but the most visible component of this particular system is a colored reporting sheet categorizing offensive behaviors and labeling student actions in the process.

In the reporting and enforcement modes, ***"unacceptable"*** offenses are always considered ***major*** and always result in the same <u>specified, serious consequence</u>. Actions reported and verified to be of an ***"inappropriate"*** nature are considered ***minor*** (the "garbage "behaviors previously referenced in this book; the ones most apt to irritate and burn out teachers) and are treated as discretionary in terms of both reporting and enforcing, with less serious consequences imposed through student participation in the resolution process. Though life-space interviewing, students very quickly begin to see a direct relationship between their actions and the resulting predictable, and meaningful consequences. For example, if a student fought (a **major offense**), suspension resulted (**specified, serious**

consequence) but if a student caused momentary chaos in her classroom (a minor offense) she might miss recess or if the student had suggested this in a previous incident--her parent might be called in for a conference.

Once such a system is operating, limits are clearly defined which allow personnel to concentrate energies on the more positive aspects of teaching and learning. Students internalize the rules quickly so little attention to control by authority is necessary.

In this book examples are given of students fighting constantly, disrespecting teachers, urinating on walls, etc. the year before this system was put in place and, within 6 months of implementation, teachers were actually spending time discussing whether or not **gum-chewing** should be put on the list!

When a schoolwide system is being considered, several issues need to be discussed first. These include agreed-upon regularity of consequences, standardization of communication, standardized record keeping, central office sanction, acceptance of proposed consequences, ongoing attention to detail—such as the color of the reporting form—and mechanisms for feedback.

While the original system was characterized by degrees of staff/student/parent participation in the development of the reporting forms and behavioral listings, adaptations to the system have shown that the system can be successfully implemented without such extensive participation. In less formal settings, the process of categorizing offenses and helping students think through consequences can still be implemented effectively. Aspects of the system that remain similar are (1) the interview (2) a recording form used only by the principal (3) establishment of an "acceptable" behavior code, and (4) designation by the principal or periodic discussions with staff regarding behaviors they would like to see extinguished.

Preplanning is necessary before the system is instituted. The style of decision making that is comfortable for the school is a major consideration. While it is possible for principals to develop their own behavior lists, reporting and recording forms, and behavior outcomes, it has proven helpful for the administrator to utilize a degree of staff/student/parent involvement. As a rule of thumb, the more involvement in preplanning, the more cooperation can be expected when the system is actually implemented, and the less revision will be required throughout the reporting years.

Typically, in schools where there is voiced dissatisfaction with the present method of limit setting, it is possible to get enthusiastic support from most of the staff.

When the system is adopted, it consists of the following elements:

- A **reporting form** in a **distinctive color**, with a method for using this form when reporting and recording "inappropriate' and "unacceptable" behaviors.
- **"Unacceptable"** behaviors **MUST** be reported by any adult who becomes aware of them and certain pre-established consequences **MUST** always occur.
- **"Inappropriate"** behaviors **MAY** be dealt with by an adult in a manner which s/he chooses. A referral to the principal is one of the several options and the consequences can be as discretionary as the reporting.
- **An interview by the principal** or his predetermined designee recording what occurred with student participation in the resolution follows the open-ended nonjudgmental fact-finding format.
- **A commitment by the interviewer to follow up** with the reporting person whether through the written report or specialized form lets the sender know what happened without interrupting class time.
- **Yearlong charting** of weekly schoolwide actions is posted prominently so all can see trends.
- **And lastly, modification of details** of the system when staff consensus is reached regarding necessary modification of administrative revision.

The following example of what we called "pink slipping" follows here with explanations of the dynamics involved:

I.M. Composite Elementary School ***PINK SLIP*** ***(front side)***

Sending person ________________ Receiving person ________________

STUDENT ________________ Date __________ Time __________

UNACCEPTABLE BEHAVIOR (It is expected that, when substantiated, this behavior will result in suspension for rest of the day and the following day. A parent conference will precede return to class)

__________ Dangerous Fighting (attack or overzealous self-defense resulting in potential injury)

__________ Vandalism (deliberate destruction of valuable property}

__________ Extortion/threatened Extortion (involving money, food, possessions)

INAPPROPRIATE BEHAVIOR (Such behavior requires special attention; consequences suited to behavior)

__________ Fighting (less severe)

__________ Insubordination (refusal to follow directions, running away from staff, talking back, etc.

__________ Stealing

__________ Disruptive behavior (Sender suggests: time-out _____ interview _____ further consequences----

________________ sexual misbehavior

________________ obscene language

__________ verbal attack

4

__________ Poking, shoving, loud noises, repeated distractions

__________ Other and Description of Incident

__________ Sender __________

When students are remanded to the office, this sheet accompanies them noting the problem. As the student relates "his or her side of the story"; it's recorded here as well as what the student suggests his or her consequence should be for this offense and any repeated offence in the future.

PINK SLIP **INCIDENT** **receiving person** __________
(back side) **RESOLUTION RECORD**

DATE __________ **time**

Name(s) **Alleged situation** **issues** **resolutions**

____

____

____

____

____

____

____

____

____

____

Parent /Guardian contact __________

Response __________

Student signature __________

Student Comments and/or Resolution __________

____

____

APPendix C

I. M. COMPOSITE ELEMENTARY SCHOOL
SERIOUS INCIDENT REPORT FORM

SENDING PERSON D. Madison RECEIVING PERSON I. M. Administrator
OTHER ROUTING PERSON(S) ——
STUDENT Mary Sweat DATE 3/3/77 TIME 9:10
HOME TEACHER D. Madison (Grade 6) (PARENTS) GUARDIAN Mr & Mrs James Sweat

THIS STUDENT IS REFERRED TO THE RECEIVING OFFICE FOR THE FOLLOWING REASON(S):

UNACCEPTABLE BEHAVIOR (It is expected that, when substantiated, this behavior will result in suspension for the rest of the day and the following school day. A parent conference will precede return to class.)

___ Dangerous fighting (Unprovoked attack or overzealous self-defense resulting in behavior which has a believable potential for serious injury

___ Vandalism (Deliberate destruction of valuable property)

___ Extortion/Threatened extortion (involving money, food, possessions.)

INAPPROPRIATE BEHAVIOR (Such behavior requires special attention. Consequences will be suited to the situation.)

___ Fighting--less severe

___ Insubordination (Refusal to follow staff directions, running away, talking back, etcetera)

X Disruptive bhavior (Sender suggests: Time Out X Interview X
Possible further consequences X)

___Sexual misbehavior

___Stealing

___Obscene language

___ Deliberate verbal attack

X Poking, shoving, loud noises, repeated distracting behavior

X Other leadership conflict with the teacher.

DESCRIPTION OF INCIDENT Mary is often at the center of attempts to disrupt our lessons. This week there has been an increasing number of such incidents. When Mary gives the signal, the class goes into uproar: everyone giggles on cue, books fall to the floor, children fall out of their seats, etc. While I write this, she is currently directing a roomful of confusion.

SIGNATURE (Sending Person) Dolly Madison

[illegible]

INCIDENT RESOLUTION RECORD

DATE 3/3/77

TIME 10:20

INCIDENT NUMBER 1

PARENT/GUARDIAN CONTACT:

LETTER —

OTHER —

RECEIVING PERSON I. M. Administ[rator]

STUDENT SIGNATURE(S) Mary Sweet

Gwen Lincoln

Arthur Van Buren

NAME(S)	ALLEGED SITUATION	ISSUES	RESOLUTION
Mary Sweet Also interviewed Gwen Lincoln Arthur Van Buren	I have randomly interviewed several of the sixth graders. They do, indeed, look to her for leadership. Mary admits "being 'in on'" the planning for a number of disruptive incidents this week. She declines to name the others involved. I have explained that I take such authority conflicts very seriously and that Mary must take the responsibility for her own involvement whether or not the teacher discovers who else is involved.	1) Misapplied leadership 2) Disruption of lessons 3) Covert insubordination	1) Mary promises to stop planning and participati[ng] in disruptions. She will cooperate with Miss Madison in finding a less tempting location for her desk. 2) Mary will report to me before she goes to class, each Friday until spring vacation, to report her progress in learning to be a helpful leader. 3) Miss Lincoln will make a daily report on Mary's behavior for 2 wee[ks]. 4) If Mary is reported aga[in] for this behavior, her parents will be notifi[ed] and she will receiv[e] a day's suspension from school.

APPendix C

Sample Incident: Mary Sweet

It is very difficult for the classroom teacher to counter this kind of disruption without predictably firm backup support. Such a leadership conflict may occur in any elementary school, particulary when the classroom teacher is lacking in authority or is frequently absent, for whatever reason. The power vacuum in such a situation sometimes encourages a determined, popular, creative child to take over classroom leadership in ways which interfere with classroom learning. Such a child rarely commits a serious breach of rules, but becomes adept at setting up clusters of distracting activity throughout the classroom. Even when most of the class members tire of the games, they are often caught up in the peer momentum and are quite grateful for the re-establishment of firm boundaries. When the school-wide report system is functional, it is possible for substitute teachers to also use the backup system in a preventive manner, even when the incidents seem trivial. Administrators often hesitate to initiate and support such a system, when seemingly trivial reports might reinforce teacher weakness and abuse of the backup system. There is a vision of a parade of children being sent to the office regularly.

In practice, there truly is just such a parade during the initiation period of the system, as children and teachers are trying out the limits; however, this heavy use of backup disappears within several weeks. Later flurries of use by a particular class or teacher can be a valuable diagnostic sign that administrative attention in needed.

Mary's principal is now alerted to the need for firmly supporting the teacher's authority for the duration of the power struggle. Since the goal involves return of control to the classroom teacher, the principal has included, in the resolution of the incident, a clearly delineated follow-up procedure for the next several weeks. It is necessary that teachers and parents understand, in such situations, that close administrative attention is not corrlated with a negative evaluation of teacher performance.

It is very likely that Mary will be sent to the back-up office again, and that several of her friends will be similarly "on report" during the next several weeks. When a classroom rebellion has gathered enough momemtum, it is sometimes necessary to meet with parents as well. The documentation which accompanies the system is helpful in gaining parental support. Misplaced leadership is often an experiment by bright, creative children, and it is helpful for teachers to utilize the system fairly early in the experimentation period, in order to prevent such children from establishing a habitually disruptive approach. The knowledge that there is firm backup for such prevention will enable the school to channel Mary's creative leadership in more productive ways.

APPENDIX: D

TALLY: SCHOOL B (Teacher rankings of serious behaviors)

Number of Responses	Mean Rank	OPINIONNAIRE
Number of Responses	Mean Rank	Teacher-described Behaviors
16	2.7	Fighting dangerously
16	3.0	Deliberate Attack or injury
1	3.0	Other (Deliberate destruction of property)
13	3.9	Sexual assault
16	4.4	Throwing Dangerously (rocks, scissors, etc.)
13	5.5	Insubordination (refusal to follow directions)
3	5.7	Disruptive behavior (loud noises, poking, shoving)
14	6.0	Extortion (threatened or actual)
13	6.0	Ganging up against other(s)
3	6.0	Threats of bodily harm
2	6.0	Inappropriate use of building/furnishings (walking on tables, writing on walls/furniture)
4	6.2	Leaving school
12	7.1	Obscene language or gestures at staff members
15	7.3	Stealing (deliberate)
3	8.0	Roaming; leaving rooms or activity
1	9.0	Insulting other students
1	10.0	Fighting, less severe
1	10.0	Deliberate messing (flipping food, spit balls, etc.)
0	-	"Cutting down" teacher's assignments
0	-	Wrestling, tumbling, Kun Fu, etc.
0	-	Lingering, dawdling outside after recess or bells
0	-	Kicking or banging on doors
0	-	Unauthorized propping of doors
0	-	Shoes and socks off
0	-	Time-out needed
0	-	Other (only one response--see above)

These items were randomly distributed in a list circulated to teachers, with the request that the teachers rank order the ten most serious behaviors, (The highest ranking was #1, and the lowest was #10.) There was 16 respondents. Items were derived from a previous brainstorming session during a staff meeting, with further access and additions to the list for all staff for a week prior to compilation of the questionnaire.

Teachers were informed of the tally at the following staff meeting and further discussion resulted in condensation and clarification of items. The building administrator was then able to achieve consensus on the final report form at the next staff meeting.

Appendix G

COMPOSITE SCHOOL "PINK SLIPS" 1974-5

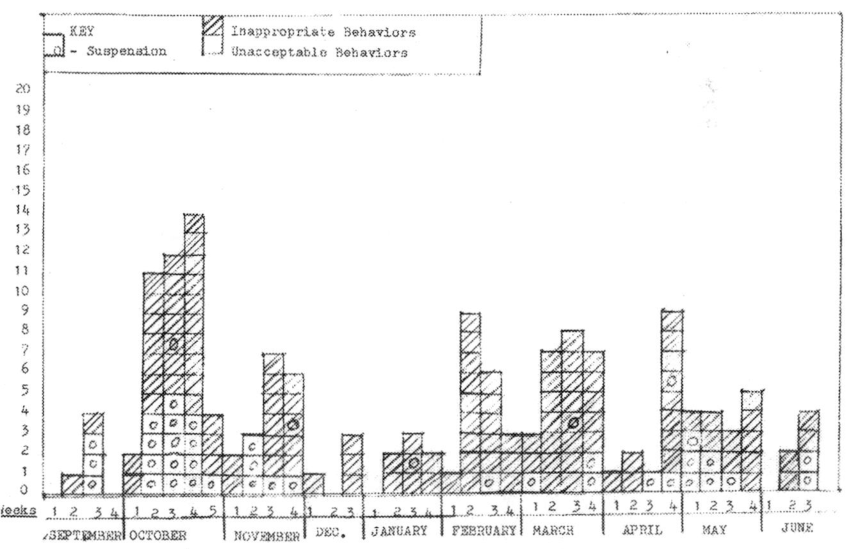

It is important to note here the regularity of consequences for legitimate reporting of "unacceptable" behavior is both the most difficult and the most necessary aspect of this program. The power of this system hinges on the principal's ability to maintain the agreed-upon consequences (e.g. suspension). There are usually temptations to "let off" a particular child (i.e. Board President's son) "just this once" or on the other hand to impose longer and longer suspensions on a child who repeatedly is sent to the office and whose family is unresponsive.

It is important to remember when consequences are discretionary for both administrator and staff and for a broad range of "inappropriate" behaviors, one of the principal's discretionary decisions may very well be to institute a one-day suspension and this fact should be understood in advance. What the system requires is a base of standardized expectations, severity of consequences is often a side issue, as is the use or avoidance of corporal punishment as a standardized consequence. Paddling—for those systems where this is a culturally approved and legitimized consequence—is left to the administrator's judgement.

Record keeping is essential. The suggested reporting sheets should contain most of the information required for such purposes. It is important the offending student be interviewed before s/he returns to the classroom and that the relevant information is recorded on the back of the pink slip. The student is read—or can read—what has been written and is asked to sign the page to indicate that s/he understands the incident is now on record. Parents are always informed of a major offense; the minor ones are generally reported only after the same kind of problem is repeated. In fact, as part of the life-space interviewing which occurs every time, students often suggest informing their parents as a consequence if their promise to change their behavior is broken. The fact that students know they've agreed to future consequences (in most cases, they suggest what should happen "next time") serves not only as a deterrent to a "next time" ***but also as a very effective teaching device increasing expectation for student ownership and responsibility for individual actions.***

Acceptability of standardized consequences is by no means easy to achieve. It is important for the principal to understand and be willing to explain the rationale many times over. It is this repetition and the rationale that eventually achieves success in communication the schools' **behavioral expectations**.

There are many attempts during the initial implementation stage to convince principals to lift consequences for "special cases" (See Stanley's story in book) or to escalate consequences for others.

In time, acceptance and consistency occur and suggestions to change the system are usually very strongly resisted by the very staff and parents who were most skeptical.

Attention to detail is also important. One of the details that has been taken seriously is the use of a ***colored reporting form.*** Staff members discover that this colored form is soon perceived as a stimulus when accompanied by a child headed to the office. Teaches and substitutes report that students settle down considerably when they merely glance toward the desk where the colored reporting forms reside.

Other details include a consistent record-keeping system and weekly notations on a cumulative chart posted in the room while staff meetings are held, serving a as a natural group stimulant. If the report forms themselves are prepared with holes punched in margins, it's easy to store them in a ring binder.

In this way, a year's records can be kept in a single binder—alphabetized according to the student's last name or according to the months of the year. If there is a tally chart in front of the binder, the incident can be tallied for charting before the filled- out form is filed. Some principals prefer to create a folder for each pupil reported and to store the forms in a file drawer. Other principals have summaries of offenses on three-by-five cards and thus can recall the information in seconds—including what the student and/or administrator suggested what should happen "the next time".

A major advantage in establishing a schoolwide, consistent approach to discipline, derives from the fact that it includes a consensual framework for viewing both consistent and discretionary consequences for undesirable behavior. This results in a sense of trust for both staff and students and frees the classroom teacher from most of the difficulties that occur when children continually test limits. Relying on a clear reporting system, teachers no longer have to emphasize authoritarian aspects of control but can now concentrate on classroom norms and foster increased responsibility and self-control in their students.

Furthermore, schools that utilize effective limit setting are perceived by visitors as comfortable, relaxed, orderly environments where children and teachers get along well with one another. Morale improves greatly and there are very few complaints from staff regarding lack of support from administrators. Principals no longer dread students waiting in the anteroom since procedures for interviewing them have been made routine and can now be fitted more easily into a busy administrative day. It is also easier for principals to leave their buildings when necessary since these standardized procedures can be easily delegate and documented. Having students sign their forms makes them increasingly aware of their actions and the life-space interviewing with active listening helps students sort out ways they might have avoided the disruptive behaviors altogether.

Students discover ways to negotiate "time outs" with their teachers and are able to withdraw more quickly from troublesome situations; they find it easier to offer genuine apologies and less necessary to appear "tough" within an environment that considers them responsible, considerate youngsters who sometimes make mistakes and who are willing to learn peaceable methods for getting along with others.

But the most obvious advantage, of course, is that a school once perceived as having "discipline problems" is now pointed to with pride as having "settled down to business". Children seem more eager to come to school—even children who are "on report" more often than others. A typical pattern is thus illustrated by one school that averaged fourteen children on report a day early in the implementation period with as many as five suspensions per week to having its average drop to one a day with very few suspensions for a period of years.

This approach was lauded by INSTRUCTOR MAGAZINE years ago and has withstood the test of time. Dozens of districts around the country have implemented it successfully.

The most rewarding part of this system of effective limit setting, however, is to witness kids working out things for themselves. It is always amazing (if not amusing) to see how many problems can be "solved" between offending parties in the two minutes it takes them to get from their classrooms to the principal's office.

Finally, the most important aspect of this system is that people working in a school regain the "rush" that comes from being better able to control their teaching environments in a positive way. Teachers who are empowered to teach rather than worry constantly about classroom control or feel embattled within their own rooms or out in the halls begin, once again, to experience the joys of the job.

Students begin to channel their boundless energies into learning how to learn and how to live in a democratic, responsible society—one in which they are personally involved in creating or maintaining themselves.

After all, it isn't the way we behave but the way we're treated that makes the ultimate difference in what we have all come to expect out of our schools. And, with this systematic approach, you, your staffs, parents, and students can expect discipline that works!

For more specific implementation, feel free to contact the author at pygmalionprincipal@netzero.net

Tips on setting up school-wide events

In all of my schools the major focus was on students, their challenges and their successes by creating and fostering school-wide activities that made school "fun" we found that students became more motivated to attend school regularly and put forth their best effort. As a surprising side effect, we also found that parents and our communities at large appreciated the services we extended to them. Whether it was a School-Wide Health Fair, Tool Day, or Vehicle Day, students eagerly learned new lexicons and greater appreciation for careers. TOAST was specifically for teachers but, ultimately and as intended, the students were the real beneficiaries. We went from 46/o of our kids in the top quartile of reading to 86% and I believe having these activities helped us reach those heights

Raising Expectations

Middle and High School students can present the biggest challenges when trying to engage their minds and enlist their cooperation during long school days. At Milan we created a systemic approach to raising our level of expectations and, subsequently our achievement. This program was well thought- and amazingly successful when all staff collaborated. Parents and students were well-informed of out expectations and the consequences if these expectations weren't met.

WAYS TO SET UP SCHOOL-WIDE EVENTS

A School-Wide Health Fair

As principal of Woodruff, Chapelle, and Ardis Elementary Schools in Ypsilanti, we tried to promote healthy habits because healthy children perform better in school and miss fewer days. Recognizing society's economic realities of high medical costs and less accessibility for the poor or medically naïve, we took the initiative in teaching health and safety to by students by encouraging them to become their own caretakers.

Since poor parents are often not equipped to get across lessons of good health and hygiene, we decided to help in meaningful ways. One of the best ways to reach kids about their health is to engage them in related activities. That's why we held school/community health fairs every year since our first one—and the first in the country—in 1974. We set up several booths in the gym and invited the public to come and learn about maintaining good health.

During that month, a variety of learning experiences was offered through a multi-agency approach. Parents, representatives of local agencies, student nurses, PE, music, art, and all classroom teachers worked together to heighten interest in preventative health maintenance, emphasizing individual responsibility. The gamut of activities ran from school-wide assemblies to puppet shows featuring handicapped students as the stars. Two highlights were a schoolwide breakfast at kickoff and a Mayoral Proclamation every year. With the help of our school nurse, Jo Ann Sheard, we set up 15 booths manned by local health agencies and professionals who contributed materials and personnel. Page 1

The Michigan Heart Association, local Red Cross, and American

Cancer Society sent free pamphlets and films and other health professionals volunteered to work in booths to excite and involve kids.

Among the most popular booths were:

- *The Weigh-In Booth.* Volunteers would weigh and measure participants and discuss their weight goals, bone structure and growth patterns
- *Guess-the Food-Booth*: Here volunteer asks kids to reach into a grocery bag blindfolded and name the food and the food group to which it belongs then discuss that food's nutrients and what it does for your body
- *The Creepy-Crawly Booth*: Teachers put bacteria and viruses in agar cultures under microscopes for students to examine. People learned what germs look like and there is a doctor on hand to explain how personal hygiene and immunization can prevent communicable diseases carried by such germs from spreading .
- *The Alcohol Truth Booth*: the volunteer at this booth presents children with facts and myths about alcohol; participants must decide if the statement is true or false and the winners get prizes.
- At other booths, students could have their vision, hearing, pulse, and blood pressure checked. Information on family counseling, drug abuse, epilepsy, and diabetes was available and referrals or appointments could be made with doctors, dentists, opticians, or social workers on the spot.
- We offered the same services to adults because we wanted our parents to begin to access sources other than the emergency rooms for their health needs.

The fair was the culmination of an **entire month's** preparation in the classroom. We had clowns present the differences between good mental and physical health, school-wide breakfasts, and school assemblies where staff dressed as vegetables and fruit yelling, "Where's the beef?" We also had the

dental mobile van service all students, as well as policeman and fireman come talk about safety and first aid. We prepared and taught lessons on nutrition, and sex ed, even spending time on teaching a whole vocabulary on emotional health.

We covered health careers one week and the human body the next. We periodically covered maturation and substance abuse throughout the month and ended with a community luncheon.

We had all staff evaluate the offerings throughout Health Month and make suggestions for the following year. Many suggested field trips to the hospital as well as visits from the Rescue Unit so we included those in subsequent years and highlighted student involvement through a school poster contests.

Vehicle Day

In two schools we celebrated an all-day extravaganza we called Vehicle Day. Hardly anyone turns their oversized playgrounds into parking lots on purpose, but we did exactly that!

The florist's van rolled in by the fire engine as a dune buggy pulled up to a dump truck. The bookmobile backed in near the street sweeper and a sheriff's helicopter hovered over a car of the future. Our local hearse vied for space with the cookie truck and the ice cream caravan made way for a pizza delivery car.

Kids honked the horns and climbed behind the controls of the cherry picker for a day they would not soon forget.

This event was preceded by weeks of preparation in the classrooms. Teachers taught language lessons built on transportation cues, "10 4 big buddy" and technology.

Students made job shields and prepared interview questions for the drivers. Younger students competed in poster contests and older students brought in family anecdotes having to do with cars and trucks. (Ford and GM were mainstays in the community).

Careers were explored: everything from pilots to entrepreneurs who sold food out of their vehicles were discussed. And a surprising side-effect, the community was absolutely thrilled to see the school recognize the importance of their common jobs.

To plan such a day, begin by asking twenty to thirty local businesses to bring in their vehicles on a specific date. Start the day with a school wide-greeting, then schedule groups of students at forty-minute intervals to climb aboard vehicles and ask the drivers questions. Back in the classroom, discuss the science and history of transportation, write up the interviews and explore the places on a map where vehicles have been. Discuss the safety precautions drivers must take, especially in inclement weather. Then draw pictures or write stories about the experiences of Vehicle Day. Lastly, enjoy the cookies and milk from the food truck!

Toast

The last school-wide event I will describe is for the adults in the building. In addition to the structured approaches already delineated in this book, I would like to briefly describe a technique for raising test scores in a building.

At Ardis we created TOAST, an acronym for **T**eaching **O**bjectives **A**nd **S**trategies for **T**esting. In Michigan, as in most states, increasing emphasis is put on statewide minimum competency tests.

Each year each districts' test scores at 4th 5h 6th 7th 10th and 11th grades are published in the local papers. Even teachers who did not agree fundamentally with these tests knew—from a practical standpoint--how we looked compared to other schools, even in our own district.

Never mind that over half of our children were on free or reduced lunch, or all of them were bussed, or a large number came from a single parent home. With 56% minority we were considered racially and economically "impacted"; English translation, our kids *were not expected* to do well anyway.

And, in fact when I arrived as principal at Ardis, they *hadn't* been doing well. Only 46% of the 4th graders had reached the top quartile in reading. Within 3 years, 86% (basically the same families) had reached the top quartile—resulting in Ardis being nominated for national honors and recognized as one of the top 20 high-achieving schools in the state of Michigan. In this book, I describe some of the strategies we used to achieve that lauded position but this one focused on the teachers rather than the students.

The teachers and I worked closely together to target our students' academic deficiencies as measured by the testing and spent a minimum of ten minutes a day in our 1-6 grades focusing on a designated objective. For example, if we had tested low in "analogies" the week we designated as analogy week meant that all teachers throughout each day (even PE, music, and art teachers) would find 10 minutes to stress that skill in the typical "lost minutes"—getting ready for lunch, switching classes, going out to recess, etc.

Each teacher also prepared, copied, or created material for the entire building on one objective on a designated week during the school year so the burden of special lesson planning was felt only once by individual teachers but the benefits were enjoyed all year by all teachers because a colleague was keeping them adequately supplied with material on each objective.

To keep within the theme of TOAST, the steering committee made breakfast and put invitations on toast in mailboxes at the end of the year as we "toasted" each other with grape juice and cheese and crackers when the results came in. throughout the year we'd "toast" students and staff in special recognition ceremonies and walls of honor.

No one had expected us to do well on MEAP **until we began to expect more of ourselves and our kids.**

RAISING EXPECTATIONS

Everybody talks about raising expectations, but few schools know how to do it. Traditionally, students were thought to intuitively know what teachers expected of them. Research shows, however, that they must be taught. This simple fact could help thousands of schools across the country improve student and staff inconsistency almost overnight.

When I was Assistant Superintendent in Milan, I helped a cadre of teachers and administrators from the middle school and high school create a model—complete with manual of instructions--on how to teach expectations to students. The credit for a lot of the work and input goes to Jean Richards, Tom Holden, Carol Reed, and principals Dave Pennington and Greg Cowgill, but the entirety of the manual can be obtained by emailing me at pygmalionprincipal@netzero.net. Below I will summarize the salient points:

The "rules" are stated as expectations because research says young people will improve their performance to meet the standards that are expected of them. Put simply, what we expect, we get.

We first informed parents, then students, of the following beliefs:

As educators, we believe students belong in school and absences and tardiness interrupt learning so need to be kept at a minimum. Removal from class or suspension from school should also be kept at a minimum, reserved for serious offenses or repeated and flagrant disregard for a safe school environment that promotes learning.

We believe we must model and demand behaviors that enable students to function effectively in an academic setting.

We will state expectations for student behavior clearly, require a strong work ethic, and commit ourselves to consistent and fair reinforcement of consequences 100% of the time.

We believe that all behavior has consequences so we will continue to recognize and applaud student achievement in all arenas. We will also respond to inappropriate behavior with measured—and, if need be, progressive—correction. Flagrant, dangerous and obscene behaviors will be dealt with immediately.

As a result of these beliefs, we have developed a set of expectations, or rules, for the academic setting which will foster student presence, punctuality, preparation, and participation in learning. These are:

- Students must be present and punctual to get maximum benefit from each class period; therefore, students will be in their assigned work areas when the bell rings'
- Students must be prepared to work by bringing only and all necessary materials to class.
- Students are expected to participate meaningfully in their own learning.

Those "rules" were explicitly explained as

1. Students will be in assigned seats before the tardy bell rings.
2. Students are expected to be prepared for the beginning of each class period
3. Students will be allowed 1 bathroom pass per marking period per class
4. Students are expected to be courteous and show respect for all individuals and property
5. Students are expected to keep class interruptions at a minimum
6. Students are expected to visit lockers when school begins to leave coats hats book bags and kept materials needed for class.

Upon the 1st infraction, students get a warning, the 2nd and 3rd infractions result in a half-hour detention while a 4th infraction means a 2-hour Saturday School. If two Saturdays have been assigned, the principal may either suspend the student or have parents accompany him/her to the class where there is a problem. Remember we want to increase school time not decrease it whenever possible.

The uniqueness of this school-wide approach is emphasized during the first week of each school year when every teacher from the PE and Art teacher to the physics lab teacher spends one full hour teaching our expectations and consequences. On the first day of class during 1st hour, the 1st rule is taught; on the 2nd day during 2nd period, the 2nd rule is taught, etc. On the 5th day students are tested on the rules and their tests are kept on file so no student can claim they didn't know the rule. Teachers also develop lessons and quizzes around the meaning of the rules and why they're important for all to follow.

Simply put, this program works because expectations are standardized and consistent. Being tardy, for example, no longer means racing for the door before the teacher closes it in one class but the student must be seated and ready for work in another. Confusion on what is appropriate behavior for students in different classrooms is lessened when teachers see they have the power to change "garbage" and nuisance behaviors by working as a cohesive team.

All administrators and faculties need to be reminded from time to time that they have Pygmalion power to make their buildings more meaningful and effective for all students who come through their school doors. It is not how they behave but how they're treated that will make a difference. Principals have the power to model leadership that "grows" adults as well as students under their care and can bring communities surrounding them to renewed life and hope. Pygmalion principles will help make these buildings premier landscapes in the educational world.

Expect the best and you'll get it; after all were dealing with the greatest profession on earth and it's up to us to keep our pupils sacred!.

ADDENDUM

PICTURES OF SCHOOL ACTIVITIES

Page 1 Woodruff students hawking the news that we were named 1 of the top 100 schools in the nation; Congressman joining us at the flag to celebrate!

Page 2 Woodruff Community Policing; Parent make and take workshops, Author Making toys for Toy Lending Library

Page 3 Woodruff staff baseball game last day, also celebrating being 1 out of 100

Page 4 Chapelle at our first Vehicle Day, also page 5

Page 6 Chapelle's Multi-Cultural Day Assembly, Tool Day and Ludington Press Day

Page 7 Ardis: Vehicle Day

Page 8 Ardis: Great Expectations, Curriculum Fair, Parent Open House 1st Day

Page 9 Ardis : Health Fair, school-wide assembly with teachers dressed as food

Page 10 Ardis: Fair of Natural Highs also page 11--had 40 choices for students

Page 12 Ardis receiving state recognition for being 1 of top 20 academically

Page 13 Milan Meets the Challenge: sample of bond issue victories

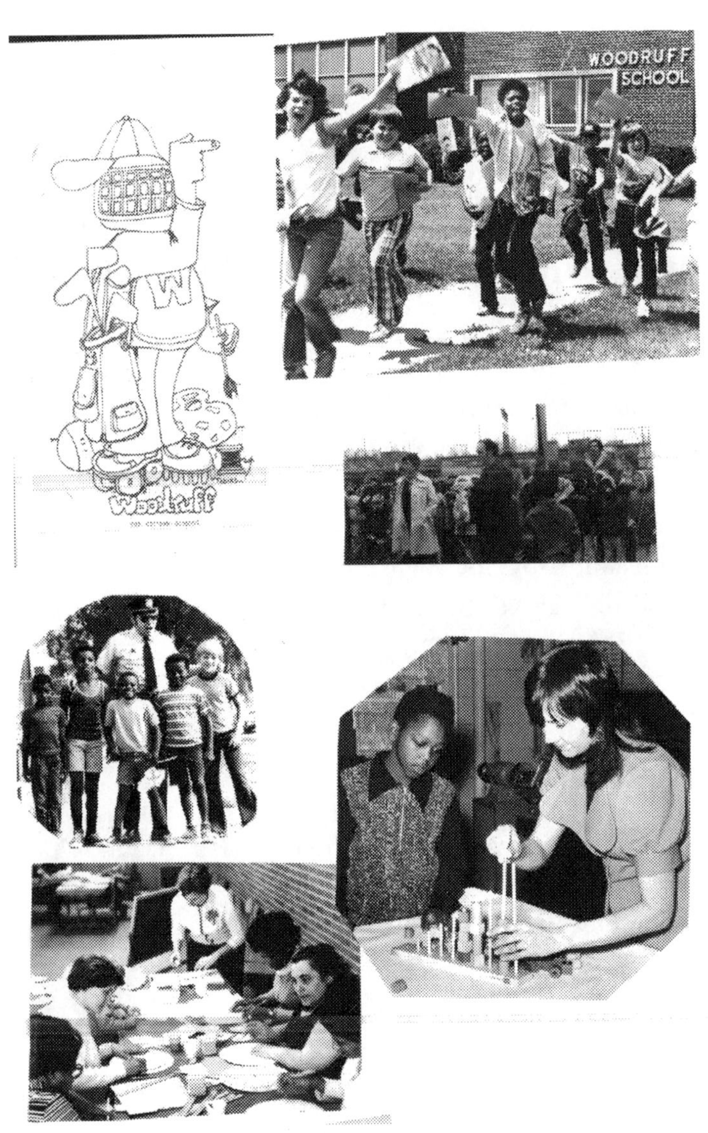
WOODRUFF
SCHOOL
Woodruff

CAREER EDUCATION VEHICLE DAY AT YPSILANTI'S CHAPELLE ELEMENTARY SCHOOL

On October 28th, Chapelle Elementary's usually quiet playground was turned into a bustling parking lot with thirty vehicles of every conceivable type and size. Farm vehicles, an army jeep, a funeral hearse, fire trucks, police cars, rescue vans, road graders, 18 wheelers, sanitation vehicles and a bookmobile all provided a first-hand look at public and private services that involve vehicles and transportation. The Washtenaw County Sheriff's helicopter even landed on the play field.

This event was the culminating activity to a school-wide career education unit that involved the study of transportation, community services and career awareness. The children researched careers, prepared reports and had language and social studies units related to the topic. The children asked the vehicle operators about their careers and the training and skills needed to perform their jobs. Both academic and career awareness were conveyed through this exciting, "real world" unit.

"The community response to our requests was overwhelmingly positive," said curriculum director Judi White. "Both public and private agencies recognized the importance of this activity for our kids." Other Ypsilanti staff members who provided leadership and support for this day were reading specialist Carla Heyn, Chapelle teacher Meg Lewandowski, Principal Pat Dignan and the rest of the Chapelle staff.

January 1981

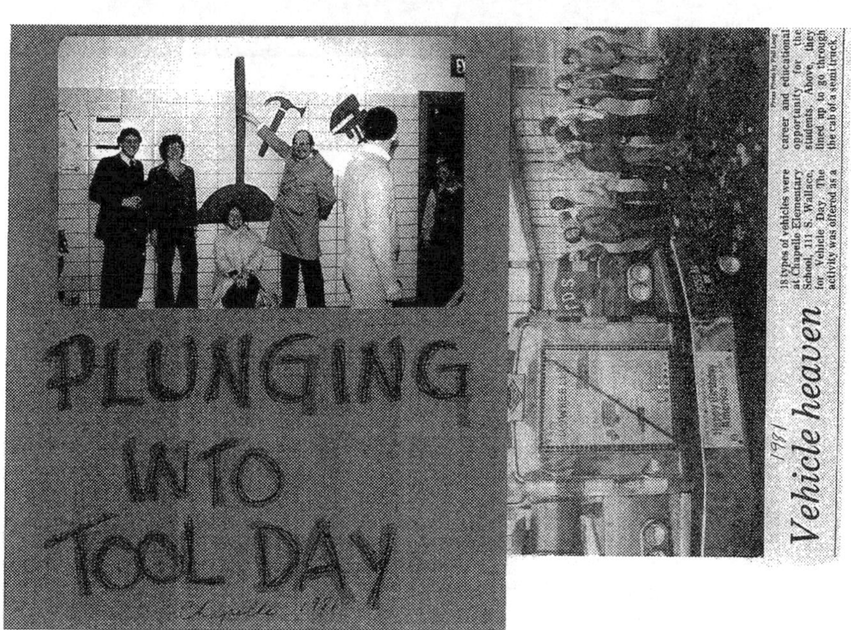

1981

Vehicle heaven

18 types of vehicles were at Chapelle Elementary School, 111 S. Wallace, for Vehicle Day. The activity was offered as a career and educational opportunity for the students. Above, they lined up to go through the cab of a semi truck.

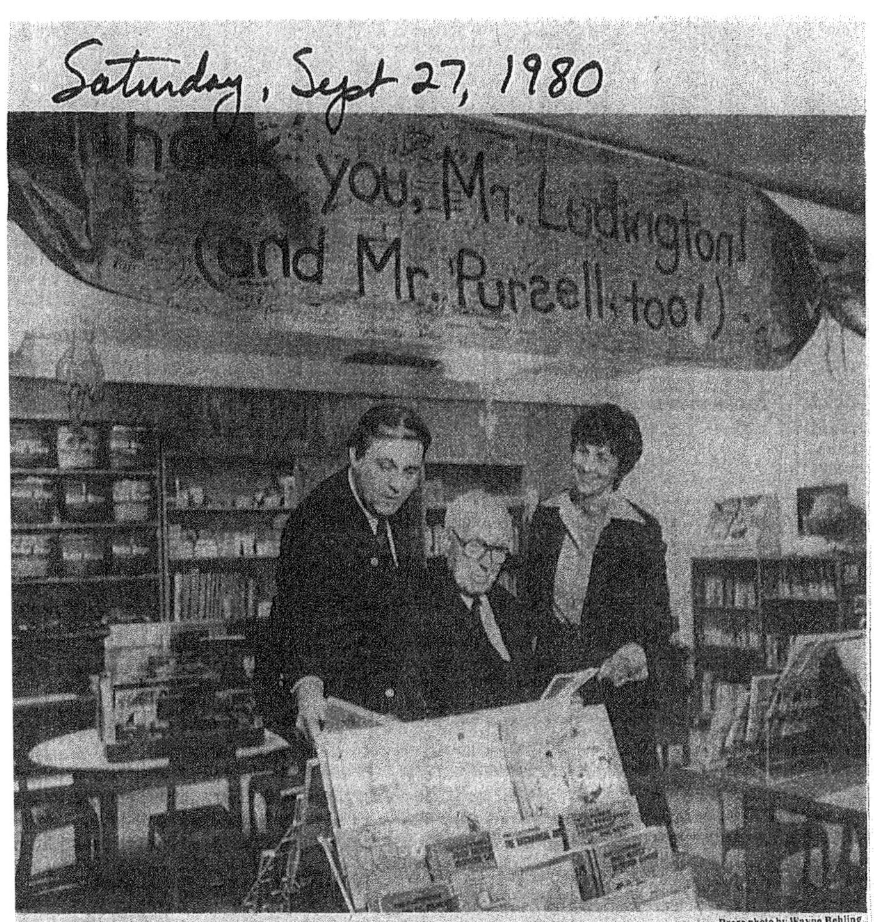
Saturday, Sept 27, 1980

Press photo by Wayne Behling

Dedication

Carl Pursell, R-Plymouth, left, Ivan Ludington, president of Ludington Press in Detroit and Patricia Dignan, Chapelle Elementary School principal, were at the dedication of the school's new reading room. Pursell was instrumental in convincing Ludington and his firm to donate books for the room.

Credit Monroe News

Instructor Magazine

AUGUST PLANNER

Great days

Get mileage from big wheels

Hardly anyone turns the playground into a parking lot on purpose, but for one day last spring Ardis Elementary, Ypsilanti, Michigan, did and attracted a lot of traffic.

The florist's van rolled in by the fire engine, a dune buggy pulled up by a dump truck, the bookmobile backed in near the street sweeper, and over a "car of the future" hovered the sheriff's helicopter.

You can plan a Vehicle Day, too. Kids who honk the horn of the police car or climb behind the controls of a cherry picker won't soon forget the experience. Not only do they learn about many careers, they are also fascinated by the technology of transportation. An added benefit comes from community members who are absolutely ecstatic over the school's recognition of the importance of their jobs.

To plan such a day, begin by asking 20-30 local businesses to bring their vehicles for a specified date. Start the day with an all-school greeting, then schedule blocks of children at 40-minute intervals to climb aboard vehicles and ask drivers questions. Back in the classrooms have kids design job shields, write up their interviews, and read about the science of transportation. (See Science Wonder Notebook, April 1986.) *—Patricia Dignan*

Round up the bikes

As soon as most kids are tall enough, they are out on the street, with Mom or Dad running along behind, trying to learn the secrets of bicycling. This is often the only bicycle safety training a child gets.

If many of your students ride bikes to school, you may want to devote a day to bicycle safety. Schools in Los Angeles often hold bike rodeos at which kids demonstrate balance, signaling, stopping, and observance of traffic signs.

The Automobile Club of Southern California also helps local schools inspect bikes for safety. Alignment, brakes, tires, handlebars, chains, seats, pedals, lights, reflectors, and locks are checked.

A mechanic or local bicycle shop owner may well be able to help you hold the same events. Lay out your bike events on the parking lot. All

for marking lines for maneuvers, a stopwatch, cardboard boxes for obstacles, a stop sign, a scorecard, and bicycle-repair tools.

The test booklet from the Southern California Auto Club offers 12 tests of skills. To test the ability to change direction quickly, set up blocks at 8-foot intervals for 40 feet. Ask the student to begin 20 feet from the first block and proceed down the line going to the right of the first block, left of the second. The cyclist passes if he or she does not hit any blocks.

To test hand signals, set up series of lines that change direction every 30 feet. The cyclist must follow the lines without excessive wobbling and use the proper signals.

To test the ability to stop quickly, draw a 60-foot line and place a cardboard box at one end. Draw

box. The bicyclist approaches from the end of the line at moderate speed and applies brakes at the 10-foot mark. The object is to stop within 14 inches from the box without skidding.

3025AX
RAW
Ford
228
Ford

NEWS PHOTO • JIM JAGDFELD

TH PARADE — No, it's not the gong show, just teachers at Ardis Elementary School in Ypsilanti ed up like food to as part of a month-long study of nutrition and health that culminated in a health n Thursday. On display for the attentive students are from left Principal Patricia Dignan as a ham-er, Alice Strawser as oatmeal, Deborah Wade-Johnson as chocolate milk, Shirley Graessley as a wa-elon, and Benni Hebrew as a box of Cheerios.

Credit Monroe Evening News

Name	Subject
Callie Meyers	Astronomy

Halley's Comet. Kids will build a comet and learn astrological facts.

Tie Dye Tulani Smith	Tye-Dying

Students will learn the African technique for dying an actual T-shirt.

Elizabeth Ramsey	Clowning

In clowning the students will learn the proper techniques for applying make-up.

Deborah Costa	Funny Sunglasses

Students will design and create their own sunglasses.

Curtis Lewis	Crayology

Students will engage in the technique for developing a coloring book.

Sharon Low	Needlepoint

Students will learn about different types of canvasses and yarns. They will create a key chain.

Meg Lewandowski	Watercolor Painting

Students will learn different techniques and create their own paintings.

Inez Weathers	Flower Arranging

Students will design their own floral corsage.

Students at school fair got high without drugs

By JOHN BECKETT
NEWS YPSILANTI BUREAU

YPSILANTI — Students at Ardis Elementary School spent all day Tuesday getting high — with the encouragement of teachers, staff and over 150 volunteers.

The highs achieved at Ardis yesterday weren't drug-induced, however. In fact, the point of the school's "Fair of Natural Highs" was to show youngsters that they possess interests and abilities that can lead to natural highs without the use of drugs.

To demonstrate that concept, Ardis principal Pat Dignan, media specialist Jovita Davis and parent Marilyn Bishop adapted a program which Bishop and Davis had seen in the Belleville schools.

The result was a day-long "fair" that allowed the school's 400 students in grades 1-6 to sample activities ranging from candymaking to cartooning, dog grooming to origami.

More than 20 presenters, not including a squad of middle school cheerleaders and a troupe of high school drama students, volunteered their skills to provide classes for the Ardis students.

Principal Dignan estimated that a total of over 150 volunteers helped make the fair possible.

Magician Daryl Hurst conducted a session on magic; Tom and Donnie Durant of Video Images Inc. helped youngsters tape a newscast; and the East Middle School cheerleaders held a clinic on basic cheerleading steps. Other topics included cooking, photography, clowning, needlepoint, science experiments, calligraphy and silk-screening.

The fair was a break from school routine, but the day had a serious purpose, outlined during a morning presentation by a high school drama class.

Playing the roles of college-bound students, the high schoolers "reminisced" about the fun, non-drug-related activities they had engaged in when they were younger, engaging in water pistol fights, pajama parties and visits to haunted houses.

"It was great," Dignan said. "The kids really loved it. Then we just repeated to kids, 'Remember, you have your own abilities to get high on.' "

The 400 youngsters moved from class to class with color-coded tickets giving them access to five sessions apiece.

NEWS PHOTO • LARRY E. WRIGHT

Dog groomer Judy Wustoff discusses her trade with Ardis students.

[S]chool overshoots fund raising goal

By LINDA HEPPE
Staff Writer

[S]tarted out as a typical [...] of a PTO raising money [pla]yground equipment.

[...] Ardis Elementary PTO [...]d that after a couple of [...] of steady fund-raising [...] be able to purchase some [...]ice pieces of equipment for [...] lower and elementary [...]rounds.

[...]y held a chicken dinner [r]aised a few bucks. The [f]und-raiser they turned to [...] sale of candy, cheese and [...]ge this fall which was [...]ted to be one of many [...]ts in the next few years. [W]hen the proceeds started [...]g in, the group found out [...]ld be the last.

[To] the amazement of parents [...] staff, the sales of the [...], sausage and candy [...]ht in enough money to [...] all of the playground [...]ment — three years ahead [...]edule.

[W]ith this kind of staff and [...] kind of parents, you know [...]ing is possible, but you [...] expect it to be possible so fast," said Pat Dignan, [...] principal.

[Wh]en Ardis was built in [...] bond money didn't cover [...]round equipment. Parents [...] up donating most of the [...]ment, but after 16 years, it [need]ed help" as Bea Kuwik, [presid]ent of the Parent Teacher [Organ]ization, put it.

[The] PTO had planned to purchase playground equipment for the lower elementary this year and equipment for the upper elementary in the 1988-89 school year.

Then the food sale netted a profit of $13,000 and the group was able to order the equipment in October. It's planning to assemble two units later this month.

The secret to the project's success was the right combination of enthusiastic parents, staff and students, according to Kuwik.

Other reasons the project was successful was because it was the first major fundraiser in a long time, there was a visible need and the PTO promised immediate results, Kuwik added.

Volunteers are being recruited to assemble the playground equipment during a workday Nov. 22.

Once kids see the playground units, it will probably be hard to keep them off. The equipment includes a slidepole, climbing tire, chinning bar, horizontal ladder, parallel bars, step tires, a log/chain climb, a clatter bridge, a crawl through tunnel, a handring set, a nine-tire net, three bannister slide, decks, a tireswing, tire trees and a turning bar.

Press photo by Mike Carden

Playground participants included: front row— Committee Chairman Donald Pennington, 3rd Grade teacher Barbara Dykman, committee member Anne Tr[...]nd [...] second row — P.T.O. President Bea K[...] [...] Grade teacher Janet Fillmore.

Credit Monroe News

Challenge:
The State has re-examined through
read.
Response:
Milan Area Schools
The bond issue will:
Vote Monday, Sept. 25
Building Together for Milan's Future
half."
over 80% of its graduates going on
and has received $50,000.00 in competitive funding
address the needs of potential dropouts.
Challenge:
The nation stresses that we are losing the best and
Response:
Milan is in the forefront in addressing hands-on science and has
MILAN AREA SCHOOLS
MEET THE CHALLENGE
Help
MILAN AREA SCHOOLS
MEET THE CHALLENGE

Milan News

et, Milan • Phone (313) 439-1802 See other Side too 25¢

Vol. 12, No. 7 Wednesday, September 27, 1995

Voters give nod to $11.6 million school bond issue by 2-1 margin

By Joy Burnett
STAFF WRITER AND
Renee Lapham Collins
ASSOCIATE EDITOR

Milan area voters sent a resounding message to the Milan Area School District on Monday, approving an $11.6 million bond issue by a 765-425 margin.

"I'm ecstatic," crowed Superintendent Dr. Patricia Dignan on Tuesday morning. "I'm probably the happiest superintendent in the universe right now."

SOME 1,195 voters cast ballots in the September 25 election, representing 16 percent of Milan's 7,409 registered voters.

"It was a really good turnout," Dignan said. "Anytime you get more than 1,000 people, it's considered a heavy turnout."

Bids went out today for "architects, construction managers, and technology experts" to get the renovation process moving.

"The board must certify the election and then the bonds must be certified, and there is a 60-day from operational to debt retirement," according to Dignan, and total tax levies will decrease over the life of the 19-year issue except in years two and three, Dignan indicated, when the increases will be "less than a mill."

Dignan indicated that some of the work could start after the first of the year.

"This is wonderful for Milan kids and the Milan community," Dignan said. "Now I feel I can leave, and that I will be leaving the district in good hands and in good shape."

DIGNAN, who announced her retirement last summer, said that the latest she planned to remain in Milan would be December 31, "but I could leave as early as next week.

"My work here is finished. The bond issue was one of my dreams for the district when I came here seven years ago," she added. "After yesterday, I think the district can make it on its own."

Dignan leads Milan Area Schools

Dr. Patricia Dignan

"If I could be superintendent of any school district in the United States, Milan is where I would choose," said Dr. Patricia Dignan, former assistant superintendent of Milan Area Schools.

So be it. Dignan was chosen to run the school district in January when long-time Milan Superintendent Clayton Symons retired after 28.5 years on the job. "Clayton Symons exemplified what a superintendent should be," Dignan said. "He fostered a sense of community, pride in the schools, and staff commitment."

"In fact, the schools in Milan have some of the most committed staff I've ever seen," she said.

And Patricia knows school staff. She's been a school administrator for 29 years and has taught Head Start, Adult Education, college and every grade, in fact, except first, second and twelfth.

Although she's spent most of her life in education, and has always wanted to be an educator, her ultimate goal is to impact people, "to turn people on to themselves, to help people grow and find resources within themselves to help them do whatever they want to do. Education means to 'draw out' and, in that sense, I consider it almost a mission to involve others in the process of growing people."

As a teacher, Dignan deliberately chose middle school as the place to draw people out. "Adolescence is a most trying time, a very confusing time," she noted. "There's an estrangement during that age when children need the best teachers, the ones who care, model, counsel, and stimulate them intellectually while embracing them, figuratively."

"During that time, parents need good teachers, too." Dignan said she realized this as a Community School Director in Michigan and California. That's when she began making home visits. "We were -- and are -- only reaching part of the child during the school day. If you can reach the family, it helps." Since that time, she's made more than 3,000 visits to children's homes.

"I made home visits as a teacher, as a principal, and as assistant superintendent," she said. "And, I hope to continue making visits as superintendent."

In the beginning, during one of those visits to check on a child who had been absent unusually long, Dignan witnessed a drug-buy going on in the child's front yard and counted 26 bullet holes in the front door. The child's father had been shot and killed during a drug deal a few nights before.

Now, whenever Dignan hears of teachers who are insensitive to children's lives outside the school day, she thinks about that visit. "Today, children have 'holes in their homes' and as much as we would like to have children 'whole' when they come to school -- they aren't."

"Schools have to develop ways to help primary care givers," Dignan said. "We need to team with all the other human services in the system so if kids come to school hungry, or hurting, they can get help. We need to work together to make life and learning better for them," she added.

Dignan plans to continue to make the best education available for all Milan students as she continues to impact education nationally. In the 1970s, she was considered an expert on school discipline; in the 1980s, she made international presentations on effective schools. As for the 90s, she is writing a book on the impact of high expectations on student and staff performance. In her spare time, she is attending law school, with the support of her husband, Patrick, and children, John, 22, and Cassandra, 21.

So, now that she has the best superintendency in the nation, how does Patricia Dignan view the job? "My job as principal was to nurture staff and students in my schools. My job as assistant superintendent was to nurture the administration and schools in the district. My job as superintendent is to help nurture the entire community since, with limited resources, we have to team whenever we can.

"We really are in a learning partnership. We need to continue to be responsive to the community and continue to build on the trust that Clayton Symons established over such a long period of time," Dignan said.

"Hopefully, the community will continue to be responsive to us. Together we can make Milan, already one of the best kept secrets in the midwest, a premier place for all learners in this partnership," she added.

Credit
Monroe News

Page 4 January 20, 1993

Pat Dignan, Milan Seem Made for Each Other

By Laurie Rorrer

"Coming to Milan was like coming home," said Dr. Patricia Dignan, Superintendent-elect of Milan Area Schools. "I can honestly say that in my 14 years of working in school systems, Milan is the best in so many ways. There is community support on all levels... it is a community that really cares about people."

Dignan has been a part of the Milan tradition for more than four years. As assistant superintendent she has introduced many new ideas and programs including a substance abuse awareness plan awarded through a Federal Drug Free School Grant.

"The drug free plan is really important to me and hopefully to the community," Dignan noted. "We hope even after the grant is over in September of 1993 that we have built a large enough following to keep the commitment going and continue the program."

One of the goals and purposes of this program is to increase the significant number of adults in the learning environment. Also, the plan aims to educate participants about the dangers of drugs and other related issues facing kids.

A program highlight for February will be TV reporter John Gross of Channel 7 who will spend a day speaking to local students. Other possible programs include a health fair in March and a summer learning program for Middle School children. Both of these events are still in the planning stages, Dignan said.

Dignan's past experiences helped her initiate new programs for Milan Schools.

Dignan began her professional education in 1959 at Bay City Junior College. Showing early promise, she was crowned Apple Pie Girl. She was the last one to receive this honor which was awarded to individuals for outstanding leadership. Dignan fondly remembers this occasion.

"When my mother called my aunt to brag," my aunt

A LOVING FAMILY: Patricia, John, Cassandra and Pat.

one of the top schools in the country with increased parental involvement.

"It was named one of the top 100 schools in the United States because of its discipline and curriculum," Dignan said.

In 1981, she was transferred to Chapelle in Ypsilanti where she spent two years. From 1982 to 1988, she was principal at Ardis. This school also made its mark. In 1987, Ardis was named one of Michigan's top 20.

"When I went to Ardis, we only had 53% of our kids

> "She meets people well, is articulate and has a high energy level. She ha[s] related very well to the staff and community. Many of the individual staff seek her help and advice."
>
> Clayton H. Symon[s]
> Superintenden[t]
> Milan Area School[s]

Credit: Monroe Evening News

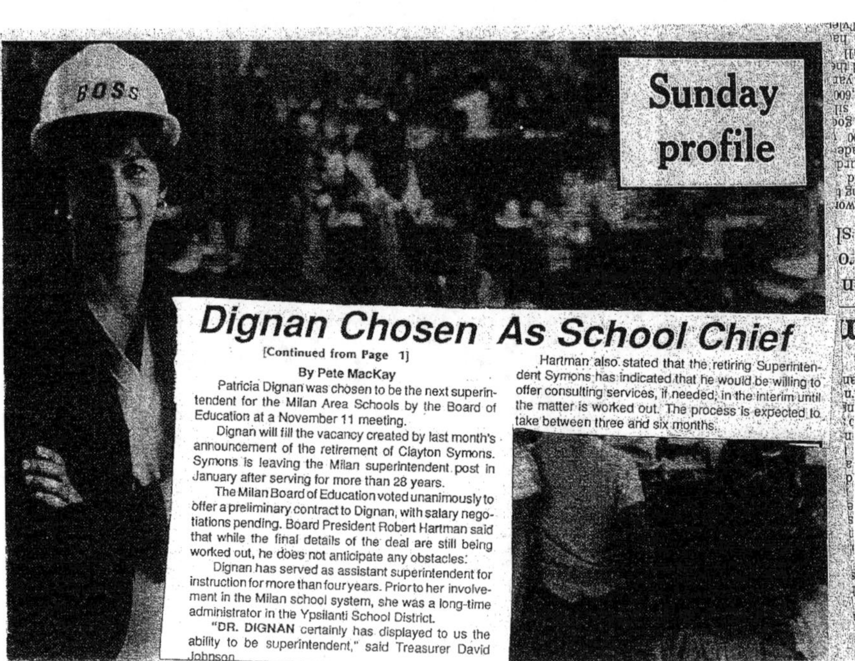

Sunday profile

Dignan Chosen As School Chief

[Continued from Page 1]

By Pete MacKay

Patricia Dignan was chosen to be the next superintendent for the Milan Area Schools by the Board of Education at a November 11 meeting.

Dignan will fill the vacancy created by last month's announcement of the retirement of Clayton Symons. Symons is leaving the Milan superintendent post in January after serving for more than 28 years.

The Milan Board of Education voted unanimously to offer a preliminary contract to Dignan, with salary negotiations pending. Board President Robert Hartman said that while the final details of the deal are still being worked out, he does not anticipate any obstacles.

Dignan has served as assistant superintendent for instruction for more than four years. Prior to her involvement in the Milan school system, she was a long-time administrator in the Ypsilanti School District.

"DR. DIGNAN certainly has displayed to us the ability to be superintendent," said Treasurer David Johnson.

Hartman also stated that the retiring Superintendent Symons has indicated that he would be willing to offer consulting services, if needed, in the interim until the matter is worked out. The process is expected to take between three and six months.

First woman named to school's top job

11/29/92

By ELISA TOMASZEWSKI
Evening News staff writer

MILAN — When Dr. Patricia J. Dignan was named Milan Area Schools' next superintendent, she became the first woman in the history of the Monroe County region to fill such a post.

She's also just the 34th woman compared to hundreds of men in the state to lead a school district.

And she wishes for the day those facts aren't so extraordinary.

"One of my biggest dreams is (that) being a woman, what I am, will not be nearly as newsworthy as what I do," the educator said in an interview earlier this week.

But in becoming the successor to Supt. Clayton Symons, who is retiring in January after 28 years with the school system, Dr. Dignan enters a profession historically dominated by men. Less than 10 percent of the state's superintendents are female.

"The reason there are so few females," she said, "has nothing to do with the scarcity of female talent," she said. "It has to do with the scarcity of female opportunities."

She considers the job the pinnacle of her career. And she knows she has a tough act to follow.

"I feel it's a real honor. I don't think anyone will replace Clayton Symons in the role he's played in leading Milan Schools to its current position of strength. The best anyone can hope to do is not to replace him, but to succeed him,' she said, adding, "That's who I feel this story should be about, not me."

Dr. Dignan's story is one of a pioneer. It began in the mid-1960s, at the start of her career in education, when she was working for Alpena's community education program.

When the coordinator's job became vacant and officials started considering her as a successor, an official suggested that a woman couldn't possibly do the job. But a well-respected principal, John Darton, went to bat for her.

Mr. Darton met with the superintendent and said, "Here's my recommendation and here's my resignation. Take your pick," Dr. Dignan recalled.

Dr. Dignan got the job, and became possibly the first woman in the nation to direct a community education program.

She left after two years, to direct Head Start and community ed programs in California. Two years later, she came back to Washtenaw, to lead its Head Start program.

After that, she worked in a variety of teaching and administrative positions at both elementary and secondary schools. She came to Milan in 1988, as Mr. Symons' assistant superintendent.

When he announced that he would leave at the beginning of the second semester, the school board talked to her about taking over. "I never turned in an application for this job," she said.

Although the board decided to hire her earlier this month, her salary and contract have yet to be decided. Right now, she's being paid about $73,000 a year. She said Mr. Symons gets about $77,000 a year.

"We honestly haven't had time to sit down," Dr. Dignan said.

The fact that the board decided to hire her without interviewing other candidates was particularly satisfying, she said. "To be considered competent enough to be in charge, it's pretty 'awesome,' to use a word the kids would use," she said with a laugh.

She doubts her gender will be an issue in Milan. "I honestly don't. Here, people are judged by what they're capable of."

Dr. Dignan, 50, sees her role as not only administrative. "I think I'm still a teacher. I think a teacher's main purpose is to help people they're working with grow and develop," she said.

The Milan district has more than 2,000 students, including those enrolled in community education. And, like any public school system, it's facing several challenges, Dr. Dignan said.

One issue is the idea that every child who attends school must go to college. It's a false expectation, she said. Some children are not suitable for traditional higher education, she believes. And, "College is not the answer to every job."

By pushing teen-agers to go even when they want to do something else, "we have set up this whole failure system."

What schools should do, she said, is make students more competitive in today's technology-saturated world. "Public schools have to recognize the role of schooling in American society has changed."

The math and science curriculum is being re-examined, but other parts of the curriculum also need to be reviewed, she said. "Schools have generally done a good job of making kids students, but that's not the same thing as making them thinkers and problem-solvers and performers."

A century ago, educators were expected to help parents instill values and a sense of responsibility in children, she said. Now, "Instead of being passive conveyors of those values, schools are being called on to lead the charge." The issue needs to be confronted aggressively, she said.

The idea of community education also must be re-examined,

See DIGNAN, Page 7B

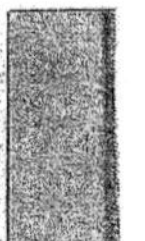

Dign

she said
for the
should

Resid
aged to
against
students

Dr. D
commu
advisor
effort.

"We (
not just
drugs,
kids alt

NEWS ROL
superinten
woman in t

The Milan
NEWS
Vol. 9, No. 50
July 27, 1994

Schools, Kids, Public Win

A lawsuit brought by a student and his parents against the Milan Schools--potentially costly in terms of time and taxpayer money--has been settled. Raymond Hoot, once a starting quarterback with the Big Red football team, sued the Milan School District last October, claiming discrimination when he was declared ineligible because of failing grades.

The following statement by Superintendent Pat Dignan to the School Board last February, and obtained by *The Milan News* under terms of the Freedom of Information Act, gives an indication of the wisdom, compassion, and concern for all parties to the suit--including the taxpayers--that the administration exercised.

ESPECIALLY SIGNIFICANT is the fact that Dr. Dignan and her family took Raymond Hoot into their own home during the summer of 1992--long before the lawsuit was initiated by the Hoots--and that Ray's emotional and academic standing by the Hoots' own admission, was dramatically improved. His learning problems, diagnosed as attention deficit disorder, underwent a turnabout, and his report cards went from failing many subjects to honor roll status.

Also significant is the settlement suggested by the administration and School Board, and finally accepted by the Hoots. It avoids a court action that could have cost the school district hundreds of thousands of dollars, in legal fees and related expenses. It also makes certain that a $5,500 trust fund--agreed to in the settlement and paid for totally by the schools' insurance company--will be used solely for Ray Hoot's training, and will be meted out only on the basis of his satisfactory performance as a student.

THE BACKGROUND OF THE SETTLEMENT is stated in Dr. Dignan's February summary to the School Board:

Today we will be discussing the fact that the federal judge, our lawyers, and our insurance company, (SEG, INC.), have requested that we settle this litigation out of court. I felt you needed to know the reasons I'will be recommending that we honor their request.

All of you know the details of the suit itself. You will recall how adamant we were not to do anything more for Ray than the law requires. You will also recall that the insurance company was willing to offer the

(Continued on Page 5)

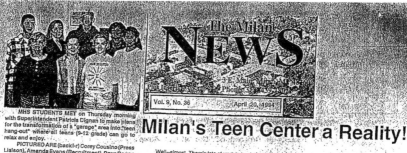

MHS STUDENTS MET on Thursday morning with Superintendent Patricia Dignan to make plans for the transformation of a "garage" area into "teen hang-out" where all teens (9-12 grade) can go to relax and enjoy.

PICTURED ARE (back l-r) Corey Cousino (Press Liaison), Amanda Evans (Recruitment), Dave Bogan (Food Procurement), and Supt. Patricia Dignan. Front Row, l-r: Dana Francis (Vending Procurement), Amanda Zurawski and Taylor Rhodes (Tutor Procurement), and Tara McFadyen who will assist Dana with vending and Amanda with recruitment. These are the students who were available to help start this project. These are NOT the only students involved. Others have helped. More are needed to help. This is a project for the entire high school student body. So, get in touch with any of the students mentioned, or Dr. Dignan, and find out what you can do to be a part of Milan's teen future!

Vol. 9, No. 36 April 20, 1994

Milan's Teen Center a Reality!

Well--almost. There's lots of work to be done, but as of 11:20 a.m. on Wednesday morning, April 13, Milan's teens have a place to call their own! Cheryl Dunn of Dunn-Well Electronics/Radio Shack informed Superintendent Patricia Dignan that the teens could use a large clear-span portion of their Dexter St. building for a meeting place. Dr. Dignan announced the good news at a meeting of the AOD Committee on Wednesday. The teens present were ecstatic--to say the least! Long, hard hours of collaboration among members of the AOD Advisory Council have paid off. Now, the long hard hours of labor really start. Last Friday evening, April 15, a group of teens, parents and friends met at the building to start the job of clean-up, paint-up, fix-up.

Christmas in April may be helping too. They have already agreed to supply the paint needed. "I know someone who will supply rock for the parking area. I know where we can get carpeting or tile. I know where we can get anything electrical at a 50% reduction." These were comments from the teen committee members. Donations of equipment, (ping-pong table, pool table, Air Hockey Game, etc.) are already coming in. And the city of Milan is helping too. They are granting a special 60-day permit to help this pilot project get off the ground.

ITEMS URGENTLY NEEDED are a small refrigerator, folding card tables and chairs, and extension cords. If you have other items you feel teens would enjoy having at the "hang-out", and would like to donate them, please call Lisa Lussier at the Milan Development Office, (439-0404) or Paulette Shores and the *Milan News* (439-1802).

The goal is to have the facility ready for occupancy within two weeks. This would allow nearly two months' use prior to the end of the school year. "It's on a trial basis," Superintendent Dignan explained. "We have it from now until June 13. It depends on what happens in those two months as to whether it continues."

The Dunns have rented the facility to the teens at a reduced rate. Funds requested and received through the Drug Free School Grant awarded earlier in the school year will pay the rent. And, Rev. Robert Goudie from Marble Memorial United Methodist Church has informed Dr. Dignan that the church will be donating $500 to help through their Ethel Richards funding.

Ideas are being sought as to how to decorate the facility, what should be included for activities, whether to charge for admission, what foods can be available, times to be open and for what purpose, etc. Get involved--be a part of history!

DUNN-WELL ELECTRONICS/RADIO SHACK, 900 Dexter is the location of the new Teen Center for Milan's high-school students.

BRIAN BLAKE, AMANDA EVANS AND AMANDA ZURAWSKI were cleaning out the building for the new Teen Center..

PADDOCK ELEMENTARY PRINCIPAL, Kathryn May arrived at the new Teen Center on Friday night with a bag full of cleaning supplies and snacks for the workers who were cleaning the building.

DR. PATRICIA DIGNAN, Milan Area Schools Superintendent, rolled up her sleeves and helped with the clean-up of the new Teen Center for MHS students. Also pictured are Amanda Evans, Amanda Zurawski and Brian Blake.

AMANDA ZURAWSKI came prepared to work-

LOCAL

We welcome your news and photo tips. Call 241-6300

Milan Schools emerges from $570,000 deficit

■ Officials say the district, under state orders to get its financial house in order, has made the necessary changes, but that long-term solvency depends on the fate of a bond issue.

By DON AYRES
Evening News staff writer

MILAN — Milan Area Schools, in the hole by more than a half-million dollars a year ago, has emerged from its deficit quagmire in half the time it had been given to return to solvency, officials say.

After an annual audit prepared by the accounting firm of Curtis, Bailey, Exelby & Sposito, PC, of Ann Arbor, the district is prepared to advise the state board of education that it is financially stable.

"We wanted to inform the staff and the community first," Supt. Patricia J. Dignan said Monday afternoon during a press conference she called to discuss district finances.

She was accompanied by Philip E. Roussey, formerly the lead auditor for Milan's auditing firm who was hired as business manager and charged with helping get the district back on track.

The district's budget for 1995-96 projects a fund balance, or money not spent, $465,889. That's a far cry from the roughly $570,000 deficit the district faced at the beginning of the 1994-95 school year.

"Dealing with a deficit is no fun," Mr. Roussey said. "We just turned over every stone. We looked at everything. We did whatever it took to make us more efficient."

When the deficit was disclosed last year, Dr. Dignan said she wasn't surprised because there had been a steady decline in the district's fund balance over the previous 10 years.

The state education department gave Milan Schools two years to eliminate the deficit or risk losing state aid, which

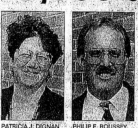

PATRICIA J. DIGNAN PHILIP E. ROUSSEY

tion is controlled by the state.

Among the measures taken by the district and the savings realized were:

- Cuts in personnel and programs, $153,000.
- Changes in bus scheduling, $100,000.
- Elimination of the community education director's position, $50,000.
- Moving to partial self-insurance, $100,000.

When coupled with an additional $201,000 received in state aid, the district finished the 1994-95 school year $175,000 on the plus side, the business manager said.

"We have had a tremendous result from an incredible amount of work this last year," Mr. Roussey said. "This is exciting, and we're going to savor the moment, but it's only going to be a moment. There are some hurdles ahead."

Mr. Roussey was referring in particular to an anticipated loss of $780,000 in annual district revenue, derived from a 3-mill enhancement millage that ends in the 1997-98 school year.

For the next three years, the district's projected fund balance will be positive, and gradually increasing. However, in 1998-99, when the enhancement millage is gone, Mr. Roussey's best financial estimate calls for a $526,000 deficit.

"If nothing else happens, in 1998-99, I predict we'll be right back at the table

healthy financially is going to take a years. One measure critical to that fin cial health, school officials say, is p sage of an $11.6 million bond issue th coming up for a vote on Sept. 25.

"We're in the black now. Only with bond issue can we stay in the black," Roussey said. "The bond issue will give the opportunity to maintain a posit position. It won't ensure it, but it's only opportunity for us to stay out of red."

The bond issue addresses essent expenditures, such as new roofs on sch buildings, replacing a 27-year-old boile the middle school or removing asbes from ceiling tiles, officials said.

"What we're trying to do with the bo issue is relieve the general fund of t responsibility for some expensive capi fund projects," Mr. Roussey said.

Paying for capital improvements wou be easier over the 12-year life of the bo rather than by one-time payments from general fund, he said.

"If I have to pay for them out of t general fund, I can't put supplies in classrooms," he said.

Dr. Dignan said if capital improveme aren't made soon, higher costs might incurred later.

"If you don't take care of a leaky ro you end up replacing the roof and the ce ing and maybe the walls," she said.

According to Mr. Roussey, over the 1 year life of the bond issue taxpaye would see an increase in taxes only in t second and third years of the issue. A in those years, the amount of increa would be less than 1 mill.

A mill equals $1 for every $1,000 assessed value of property.

For the owner of a $100,000 home, tax in the second and third years would raised by about $50, Mr. Roussey said.

After the third year, the levy woul gradually decrease from 6.49 mills to 3. mills in the 12th year.

Residents currently pay 5.5 mills, 2. mills for operations and the 3 enhanc

To the Editor,

BRAVO! Your paper has finally made this ridiculous lawsuit two-sided! It's about time we knew the school's side of the story.

I found myself amazed, that a school could do so much for a student, (even as far as Dr. Dignan letting Ray live with her family for the summer to help him) and then be sued by the Hoots for not giving enough?! Wasn't it going to be Dr. Dignan who would be jailed for contempt when Ray still wasn't allowed to play football? What a way for the Hoots to say thank-you, Dr. Dignan! And, weren't they only thinking of themselves when they wanted Ray to be allowed to play football, when it meant forfeiting the season for the other players, some of whom were seniors and might not be playing again!?

WHAT A WONDERFUL SCHOOL to do so much for a student. We should all applaud their hard work and unrewarded efforts.

The *Milan Leader* said that Mrs. Hoot said that "they did not benefit in any way." Well, they got $5,500.00 worth of education for Ray that won't come from their pockets. We, on the other hand, pay for our children's college with money that we worked hard to earn. So, I definitely believe they benefited!

There is one thing I don't understand. The Hoots admitted in Dr. Dignan's report that they were living in the Dundee school district and Ray was attending Milan schools. Excuse me, but shouldn't the Hoots be writing two checks out? One to Milan schools for tuition and one to Dundee schools for not letting them collect the funds from the government due to them for a student living in the district and suppose to be going to that school? They must have known it was Dundee schools when they moved there? Right? And for living in another school district and not paying tuition, Milan lost more money, another benefit they received by not giving the correct address.

ONE FINAL THING which was quite confusing as I read it. The Hoots told Dundee schools that "Ray frequently skipped school which resulted in summer school". What did this have to do with Dundee? He was skipping school at Milan since that's where he was going to school! How could they know he would become a "drop-out" from there if he did not attend that school? How could they make a statement without letting him attend there to find out! I know people who have attended Dundee schools with the pride of a quality education and great pride in a community with a wonderful school system. I see this as shunning Dundee, suing Milan and showing us that nothing seems to be good enough by their own admission. If the Hoots didn't believe that Milan was giving Ray a "quality education" for all these years, that they claim he had problems there, why would they be so set on his attending Milan schools and not trying somewhere else? This to me seems to be a rather large contradiction in the statements they have made to the press, and the schools. Maybe, now, the people of Milan can look at their schools with the pride of knowing that their teachers and administration give their all for our children.

Name Withheld by Request

Credit: Monroe News

PARENTAL TIPS

Having hosted hundreds of parent classes and school-wide workshops over a 50 year career, these are just some examples of my suggestions for parents. Ranging from pre-school through high school, these activities were considered helpful and more are available upon request at pygmalionprincipal@netzero.net.

<u>A TEMPLATE FOR DETERMINING THE "RIGHT" SCHOOL FOR YOUR CHILD</u>

<u>By Dr. Patricia J. Dignan, Consultant on Effective Schools</u>

There are several factors to consider when evaluating school effectiveness and efficacy for families. Some of those factors are objective while others may be subjective but all should be viewed with a particular child's best interest in mind.

A school that "fits" one child well may not necessarily "fit" all children equally well due to the varying levels of skill, age, and interests of children within the same family.

When determining a proper "fit", a child's preference, personality, potential, and learning patterns should be taken into consideration as well as practical concerns for parents such as distance, cost, curricular, and extracurricular opportunities—including availability of sports where applicable.

Opportunity to progress through the same school is a plus for those students for whom change is difficult and the possibility of siblings attending the same facility should be strongly considered not just for parental convenience but also for shared experiences between brothers and sisters.

A school's reputation should also be viewed as an indicator of past success or failure rather than a guaranty of excellence due to the fact that it often takes 3-5 years for an institutional reputation to keep up with reality and parental levels of satisfaction often reflect the child's success rather than the school's success as a whole. Generally, curbside appeal reflects the emphasis on cleanliness and pride a district harbors towards its schools. School cultures which fix problems like broken windows immediately also tend to echo the immediacy a school or district administration views problems and remediates them.

Lastly, parents and children should feel welcome and safe in the school of their choice. Schools should have a zero tolerance for bullying and harassment and should provide mechanisms and strategies to keep children from being scape-goated or left behind by their peers.

Some objective data to use when determining the best school for your child:

- **Kindergarten "round-ups" and assessments used**
- **Length of day**
- **Parent involvement opportunities**
- **Facility age and activity appropriate**
- **Options available for fine and gross motor activities**
- **Specialists who are certified at the appropriate age and grade level**
- **Test scores, including ACTs and SATs at the high school level**
- **Advanced coursework**
- **Honors and AP classes for high school students**
- **Art and Music Opportunities**
- **Foreign Language offerings**
- **Diversity of staff and students**
- **Certification and experience levels of teachers**
- **Curriculum alignment**
- **Extended and Accelerated Learning Opportunities**
- **Level of parental satisfaction surveys**
- **MEAP scores**
- **Michigan Report Card Assessments**
- **Nurse, health resources**
- **Parental involvement**
- **Quality and age of facilities**
- **Technological sophistication**
- **Sports and extracurricular offerings**
- **Standard and Poor ratings**
- **Student attendance and drop-out rates**
- **Student teacher ratios**
- **Graduation rates**
- **College acceptance rates after high schools**
- **Vocational and trade opportunities**
- **Counseling and career services**

Discussed with prospective client and other parents April 7, 2015

WELCOME BACK!

"But if I go every day, won't I wear out my welcome?"

INTRODUCTION

Math

Basic arithmetic is a necessity in life. The check book, the purchase, the recipe all demand some arithmetic knowledge. Everybody has this knowledge to some degree. It is the base from which future engineers, physicists, economists, architects and store clerks are born.

Parents can help students prepare to be unafraid of arithmetic; to get excited about numbers and to set the stage for a healthy beginning.

Mathematics is essential to understanding the world around us. Constructing the Empire State Building or the Renaissance Center demands the same basic arithmetic of a first and second grader.

Mathematics helps us in logic, in comparisons, and in assessing progress.

Children can feel successful in learning basic mathematical patterns and skills if well motivated.

Make activities fun. Counting from 1-100 is not as beneficial as being able to identify patterns.

Teach children to:

1. **Sort** - Division
2. **Compare** - What weighs more, a pound of lead or a pound of feathers?
3. **Number specific commands** - bring me two apples
4. **Memorization** - counting in rhymes/stories or rhythm tables
5. **Ordering** - relationships
6. Ask the principal for the math curriculum for your child (Grades 1-6)
7. **Estimates** - travel in car, calendars
8. **Budget**

FAMILY MATH GAMES

1. Have your children keep a "checkbook" like record of their allowance.

2. Follow baseball statistics.

3. If each child does a certain chore and they rotate - help them record how often each child does each chore in a month.

4. Who uses the bathroom the most in the family? Keep a record and work it out to percentages.

5. The family can walk, bike or jog together - How many miles per minute do they do and who is the fastest?

6. Do a pie chart graph for how much of your day you spend eating, sleeping, watching television, etc. Compare within the family, or between families.

7. T.V. - What is the most popular program the family watches?

Number Fun

Addition	Subtraction	Multiplication	Addition	Subtraction	Multiplication
5	6	14	38	13	20
7	4	49	30	18	35
10	15	54	24	43	55
20	30	10	16	68	72
17	22	25	12	4	60
33	11	81	8	2	48

RULES

1. X = Johnny; O = Susie.
2. What 2 numbers make this number.
3. Wrong answer gives his mark to other player.
4. Winner has the most squares.

Compliments of Ardis School Staff Ypsilanti, Michigan September '84

HOW PARENTS MAY HELP

Arithmetic

1. Let your child help you--
   Double check your shopping list.
   Find your train on the timetable.
   Help measure for a do-it-yourself project.
   Figure cooking recipes.
   Keep track of oil, gas, mileage, on trips.
   Plan the route on a road map.
   Check the temperature.
   Read the barometer.
   Help make out deposit slips.
   Check your canceled checks with you.
   Go over floor plans of new house or camp.

2. Give him numbers in his play time--
   Puzzle books and dominoes.
   Quick mental drills with number facts.
   Card games concerned with numbers.
   Brain teasers and magic squares.
   Word puzzles involving number concepts.

3. Don't pass your dislike for mathemetics on to your child--you will solve nothing by telling him you hated fractions too.

4. Help him to see ways mathematics is used in the modern world--
   Making tall buildings stand up.
   Rockets, jets, and space flights.
   Building roads and bridges.

5. Help him to understand big numbers--
   How big is a million?
   How long would it take to count to a billion?
   How big would a pile of a million dimes be?

6. Help him solve simple problems.

Reading

1. Make your house a house of books. If you are a TV bug rather than a reader, your child is apt to be one also.

2. Start with books that center around your child's interest.

3. You didn't get upset because the neighbor's child got a tooth before yours. Remember reading skills are not all developed at the same time.

4. Introduce your child to the library, but if the library is to be of lasting value to him, you must use it too.

5. Give books as gifts for birthdays, Christmas, and so on. (Ask librarian or teacher for ideas)

Social Studies - Cont'd.

8. Encourage a hobby that will help him build social studies concept; for example, stamp collections, flags, travel posters, dolls in native costumes, foreign pictures.

9. Help him to judge people individually. (Avoid prejudices. Control your own thinking remarks in front of the child.)

10. Take the child with you on trips whenever possible. Visit important places en route and give him a notebook to jot down impressions and discoveries.

Science

1. Develop a scientific interest--if your household appliances are mysteries to you, your child may have the same point of view.

2. Let him be a collector--a little dirt is a small price to pay for intellectual curiosity. Provide a place for the collection.

3. Be able to take cruises to outer space with him--be conversant with rockets, jets, missiles. A simple telescope is a good investment; charts of moon and stars are good wall decorations.

4. Use Christmas and birthdays to advance science--give scientific toys and science books, both fact and fiction.

5. Provide opportunities to experiment--weather sets, simple chemistry sets, erector sets, photo-developing materials, do-it yourself kits. Provide old clocks, radios, motors, and so on, to take apart.

6. Encourage nature study--learn names and location of stars, geology of area, plant life, bird and animal life around area. (Know these yourself)

7. Invest in an inexpensive microscope.

8. Subscribe to one of the children's scientific magazines.

9. Watch together some of the fine science programs on T. V.

10. Visit scientific attractions--museums, zoos, planetarium, industrial plants, and so on.

11. Have some backyard science--a bird feeding station, a rock garden.

12. Make science part of your vacation--look for fossils; study the rocks, fields, shore, mountains, erosion; visit mines, quarries, industry; look for new plants, birds, animals.

13. Discuss the scientific aspects of the day's news.

14. Help your child develop a scientific attitude. Encourage him to ask how and why. Have him seek facts to prove his statements, list evidence, draw conclusions.

This supplement is a follow up to our November publication. For those parents who are interested, we present suggestions for activities you might do with your child at home during the winter months. The ideas we cover here, will strengthen the twelve (12) readiness areas mentioned in the earlier booklet.

You as parents have a tremendous responsibility to provide the necessary guidance and communication for your child which will help him achieve ultimate happiness and success.

Child rearing, as you well know, is not a simple endeavor. It takes a great deal of patience, understanding, and a huge amount of work to feel secure in the belief that the child will grow up to be a constructive and happy adult. It appears, therefore, that the parents' responsibility is to mold a child into one who will become an independent adult who can function autonomously.

As parents you are aware that all children require great amounts of love, attention, affection, encouragement, a listening ear, self-respect and someone to copy, as well as the right to make mistakes, understand limits, suffer consequences, and to have fun growing up.

Guiding your child's development is not a skill which comes naturally to most parents. However, this skill can be acquired if some basic principles are followed.

1. Learning proceeds from the concrete to the abstract. Children learn numbers from having things to count such as apples or oranges. Later a number symbol can stand for this experience. Use material objects in place of abstract words as a beginning point.

2. Start at a point where success is easy and rewards can come quickly. Success is a better teacher than failure and defeat. Develop confidence. If he begins to fail more than succeed in the task you are teaching, always go back to a point where the child can be successful.

3. Provide a variety of experiences on the same theme. Large muscle development, for example, can be improved through a wide variety of children's games.

4. Move slowly and review frequently. Learning does not occur as a smooth upward curve. It involves backward movement, and at times plateaus where little or no progress may be apparent. Do not become discouraged.

5. Children change. Their behavior moves through periods of growth and smoothing out followed by a breakup and reorganization in preparation for the next stage. These cycles are as short as six months for the younger children. Take into account that the cooperative child of today can become the testing, independent, uncooperative child of tomorrow as a result of growth alone.

To help you judge your youngsters skill in the areas mentioned, you may want to ask him to try out the task listed in front of each area. First read through the exercise yourself and prepare the necessary materials ahead of time. If your child has trouble with any of the tasks involved, then follow through with the activities listed.

I. Motor Skills involves an awareness and control of the body in space. Development of a sense of balance is basic to most other motor activities.

Task 1 - Standing Balance - Basic skills involved: motor coordination.

Have your child stand arms crossed over his chest. Ask him to raise one foot while you time him in seconds. Stop timing when his raised foot touches the floor, the heel of his balancing foot moves, or his arms are extended to regain balance. Have him repeat the procedure on the other foot. Expected performance:
Kindergarten, 10 seconds on each foot
First grade, 20 seconds on each foot

Motor Skills Activities

1. Practice standing on each foot. Vary the position of hands (at side, on chest, on head, etc.). Do with eyes open and then closed, which is very difficult. Balance on tiptoes.

2. Balance in an all-fours position. Tell your child to put both his hands and his feet flat on floor. Have him raise left hand, right hand, left foot, right foot. Then, both left hand and left foot, right hand and right foot. Then, left hand and right foot, right hand and left foot.

3. Exercise on balance beam. This can easily be constructed with a 2 x 4 piece of lumber supported by a notched block at each end. Blocks can be notched so board may be used at either 2 or 4 inch width.

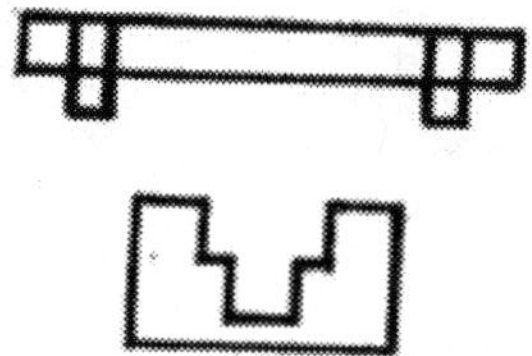

Have your child walk across the beam slowly, feet placed closely together. Walk forward, backward, and sideways. Walk with arms in various positions or carrying things. Walk and turn in the middle, or walk turning on each step. Walk on tiptoe.

4. Hopping games. Play hopscotch, or hop following a pattern on the floor.

5. Balance on three-foot beach ball or barrel. Have child balance while lying on his stomach, then on hands and knees, finally on knees alone. Rock the ball gently while your child is on it.

6. Walk on wooden block stilts; jump on pogo stick.

7. Rolling activities. Roll down hill. Roll your child out of a blanket. Turn somersaults.

II. <u>Visual Perception and Eye-Hand Coordination Skills</u> involve the ability to discriminate various shapes and coordinate vision with movements of the body. The child needs to be aware of the difference between a circle and a square and a square and a rectangle. While he may not know the alphabet yet, he can likely tell that the letter "c" has a different shape and pick it out regularly from an "e" or an "o".

<u>Task 2</u> - <u>Copying Lines and Forms</u> - Basic skills involved: eye-hand coordination, visual perception. Before you begin, take two sheets of unlined paper, approximately 8 1/2 " x 11". Draw lines dividing the paper into fourths, front and back; then draw the following designs in the upper squares only, leaving blank squares underneath for your child to make his copy in during the test.

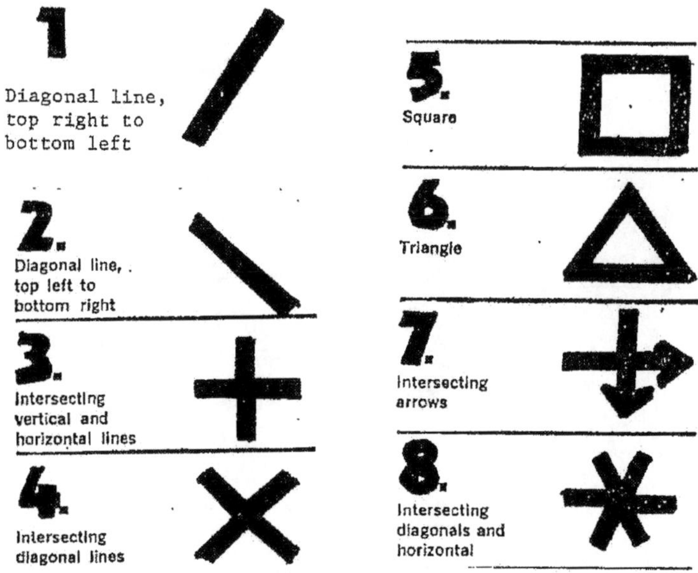

The lines your child has drawn should be straight and should run in the same direction as the lines in your model. The square and triangle must have the correct number of sides. Expected performance:

Kindergarten, 6 correct
First grade, all correct

Visual Activities

1. Play ring toss, drop clothespins in bottle, or throw beanbag in wastebasket.

2. Bounce a large ball back and forth, play catch, or bounce the ball off a wall. Try this with one eye covered with a blindfold, then the other.

3. Hit a swinging tetherball with a stick. Mark the part of the stick you want to contact the ball.

4. Play croquet, toy golf, badminton.

5. Play toy pinball games in which child rolls a ball or marble through a maze. Roll a metal washer around hangers bent into various shapes.

6. Play with beads to string; construction sets; puzzles; pegboard; pick-up-sticks, jacks.

7. Trace large form-board shapes, pictures, shapes, letters.

8. Emphasize staying within the lines in coloring books.

9. Cut out pictures and shapes and paste them.

10. Connect dot and maze puzzles.

11. Make two sets of cards with various shapes or letters. Have your child match identical cards.

12. Get two checkerboards and place them side by side. Put one checker on your board and have your child put a checker on the same square on his board. Use more and more checkers and have your child reproduce your patterns, putting his checkers in the same squares. Easy beginning patterns are vertical and horizontal lines, diagonal lines, and intersecting lines.

13. Do the same activity with two pegboards.

14. Arrange straws or toothpicks in sequence, some vertical, some diagonal, some horizontal. Have your child duplicate the sequence.

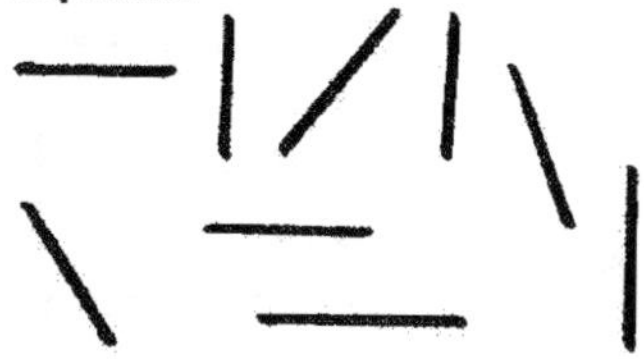

15. Make four, six, or eight dots on a sheet of paper. Then connect two, three, or four of the dots. Give your child a sheet with unconnected dots and have him reproduce yours.

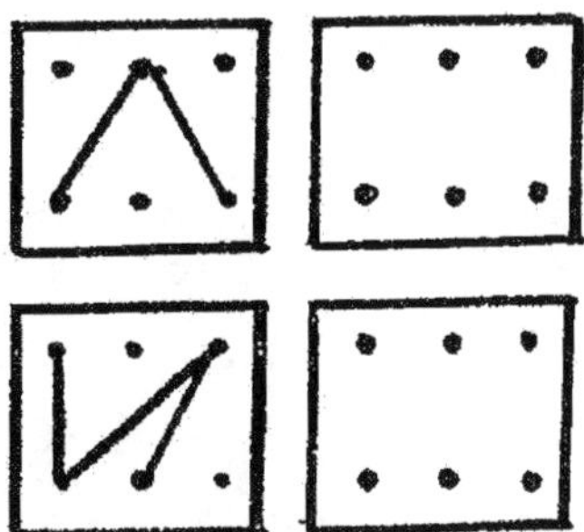

16. Make a page with circles or squares divided into fourths. Color one or two segments of circle or square and have your child color one indentically.

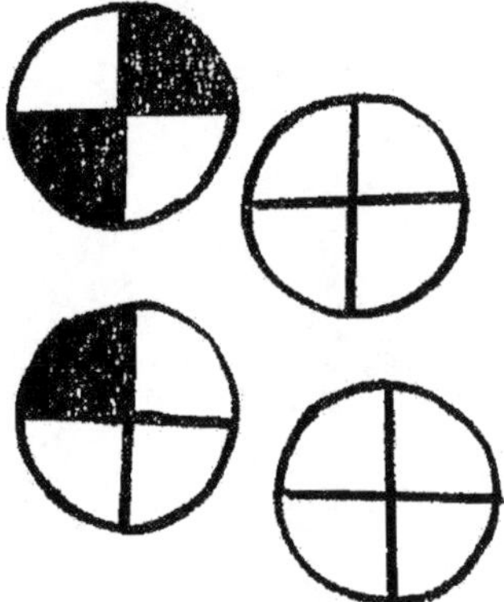

17. Make up a sheet with letters of the alphabet mixed in correct and rotated form. Place correctly oriented model at top and have your child circle or trace all other correct letters.

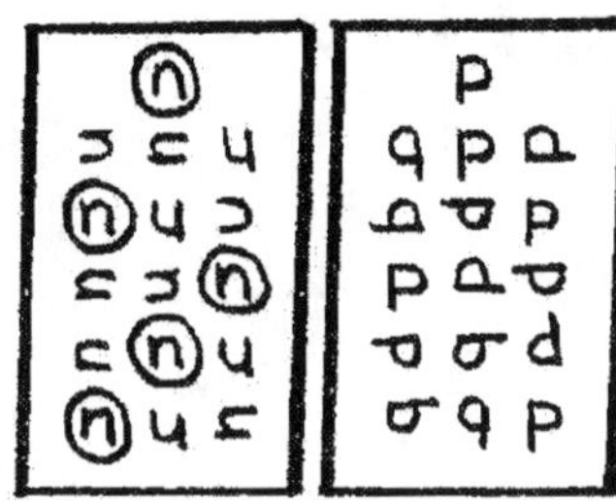

18. Have your child match identical words. Use short words with different sequences of letters or rotated or look-alike letters as unlike words. (Your child does not need to read the word; this is purely a matching skill.)

bat:	tab	bat	dat
no:	no	on	uo
was:	saw	mas	was
do:	do	bo	od

19. Let him help you sort the laundry--putting together the socks that match by size or color, for instance. If he has brothers or sisters, let him judge which things belong to which child according to size.

20. Give him a pile of buttons to sort out by shape, then color or size.

21. Let him help fold towels, sheets, and washcloths into triangles, squares, rectangles. Have him see how many things he can find in the house that are shaped like a circle, square, triangle, or rectangle. Use these names for the shapes as you discuss them with him.

22. Play a game with him in which you make a circle, square, triangle, or rectangle out of clay. Have him close his eyes and feel the figure and tell you what it is. If he is wrong, have him look at it, feel it, and say it. Then try again a little later. Let these things come naturally. Don't push.

23. For those of you whose child is in school and is not learning the sight words, have him make the word out of clay, close his eyes, and trace each letter with the fore-finger of the hand he uses, saying each letter and then the whole word. Do this eight or ten times. Then see if he can write the word without looking at it. Later, see if he can tell you the word when you show it to him.

24. Always be sure the child is looking directly at you when you give him instructions. You must have his undivided attention.

III. Auditory Discrimination is the skill necessary to hear differences in sounds. Can your child identify animals he knows by the sounds they make, does he recognize the different sounds of familiar musical instruments?

Task 3 - Detecting the difference between words that sound similar. Basic skills involved: auditory discrimination, attention.
Tell your child you are going to say two words, and he is to tell you whether the words sound the same or different. Practice with the following pairs of words until he understands the task.

1. Can...kite
2. Cat...cat
3. Walk...walk
4. Ball...ball

Then continue with these test words.

1. Ban...pan
2. Game...came
3. Man...man
4. Ram...ran
5. Pet...peg
6. Bat...bat
7. Pan...pen
8. Ten...tin

Expected performance:
Kindergarten, 5-6 correct
First grade, 7-8 correct

Auditory Discrimination Activities

1. Have variety of noisemakers such as a horn, bell, and whistle in front of your child. Let him hear each one. Have him close his eyes while you play one. Then have him open his eyes and identify it.

2. Identify animal sounds on tape or record.

3. Experiment with tones, using water glasses filled to different levels. Have your child close his eyes while you strike two glasses or the same one twice and have your child respond "same" or "different."

4. Have your child think of rhyming words. ("What rhymes with cat? Does rat rhyme with cat? Does bear rhyme with cat?")

5. Have your child match pictures of words beginning with the same sounds. (Show pictures of a car, cane, and rabbit and say, "Which two go together, which two start with the same sounds if necessary.)

6. If you are making a salad or a casserole dish, tell him what you are going to put in it. The list of things should be small to start with and gradually increase. Have him watch you. Purposely leave out something and see if he can tell you what it was. Make your list longer and leave out more things each time you do this.

7. Take your child to the grocery store with you. Give him one or two things to remember for you. (Make them something he likes.) You can start out by having him tell you the things he is remembering for you. Later you can let him get the things himself if he is old enough. Gradually add more things for him to remember until you reach about eight items. This will take quite a long time and must be done consistently.

8. Tell him or show him someone's phone number you want to remember. Wait five minutes or so and ask him to tell you what it was. If he cannot remember, tell him or show him again, and start all over. Put him in charge of remembering numbers for other members of the family. Ask him for the number when you want to call someone.

9. Have him help you remember things-such as what day or time your dental appointment is, a friend you must call, something you need to tell another member of the family, that you need to change the oil in the car or get gas.

10. Tell him the street and address of someplace you are going. It will be his job to remember it for you.

11. Put him in charge of remembering the birthdates, anniversaries, and so forth of relatives and giving you notice when to send a card or gift.

12. For the activities in which he has to remember certain dates, get a calendar. Show him each of the dates you want remembered; let him mark that date however he wants to on the calendar. Then give him the calendar. Tell him that it is his, that he must

be careful not to lose it, and that he must check with it in order to remind you of the things you need to know. Make it clear that this is his responsibility, and that you are going to erase these dates from your mind completely until he lets you know what to do.

13. Ask him to be able to tell you at the end of the day-perhaps at the dinner table or when preparing for bed-one piece of information that he has heard that day. The source is not important. It could have been something heard on television, something heard from an adult or a friend, or something learned in school. This may help him to form the habit of listening to what people say; it may also help him to learn to judge what is important to remember and pass on to others. It can help him to feel that he is a part of his family because he has something to say. Of course, his family must cooperate by giving him his chance to speak and by listening to him.

IV. Visual-Memory is the ability to recall what has been seen. Can your child draw designs or symbols after a brief look at them, or recall the furniture in a room with his eyes closed? In beginning to read, a child's ability to recall words by sight is greatly influenced by visual memory.

Task 4 - Duplicating a sequence of shapes from memory. Basic skills involved: visual memory, visual perception, concentration. Use six unlined 3" x 5" index cards. Make circles on two cards, squares on two, and triangles on two. Give your child one of each, keep a set for yourself.

Place your circle on the table. Tell your child, "Put the card you have that is just like this one under mine." Then put down your circle and square next to each other. Tell your child, "Arrange your cards just like mine." See that he puts down the circle and square in correct order. Now tell him to close his eyes. Lay down your square and triangle. Have him open his eyes and look at the cards. Then cover them completely with a piece of paper and say, "Now arrange yours just like mine." If your child lays down the wrong cards, or if they are in the wrong order, show yours again and help him correct his error. When he understands this procedure, begin the exercise.

Give your child one chance on each of the following sequences. Let him look at the model for a couple of seconds before you cover it.

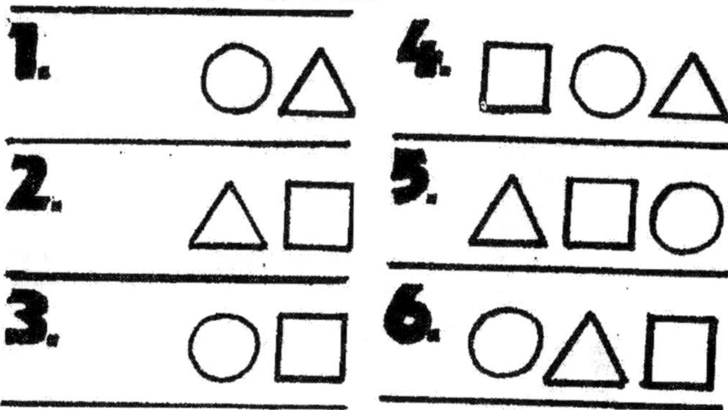

Expected performance:
Kindergarten, 4 correct
First grade, all correct

Visual Memory Activities

1. Have your child close his eyes and describe his clothing, the room, or a picture.

2. Place small objects in front of him. (a button, penny, an eraser). While he has his eyes closed, remove one item and place it in a box containing other objects. Your child must find the object and put it with the others.

3. Arrange a bead pattern on a string, show it to your child, remove the beads, and have him rebuild the pattern from memory. Gradually extend the length of the pattern.

4. Put some change on the table in a definite order, say, first a penny, then a nickel, a dime, and finally another penny. Cover and have your child reproduce the sequence.

5. Draw a sequence of shapes, numbers, or letters. Cover and have your child draw an identical sequence. Begin with two shapes.

Give your child one chance on each of the following sequences. Let him look at the model for a couple of seconds before you cover it.

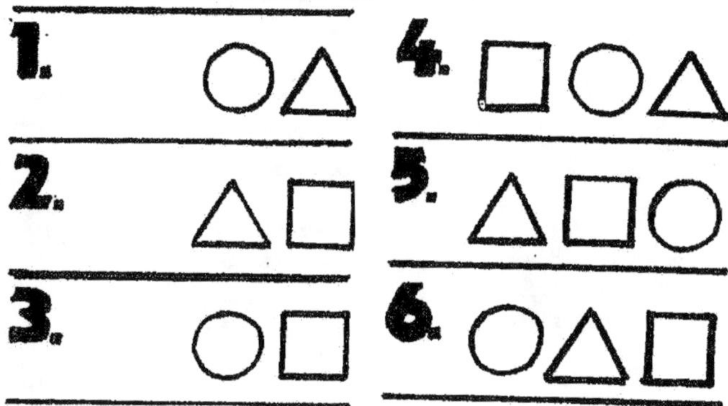

Expected performance:
Kindergarten, 4 correct
First grade, all correct

Visual Memory Activities

1. Have your child close his eyes and describe his clothing, the room, or a picture.

2. Place small objects in front of him. (a button, penny, an eraser). While he has his eyes closed, remove one item and place it in a box containing other objects. Your child must find the object and put it with the others.

3. Arrange a bead pattern on a string, show it to your child, remove the beads, and have him rebuild the pattern from memory. Gradually extend the length of the pattern.

4. Put some change on the table in a definite order, say, first a penny, then a nickel, a dime, and finally another penny. Cover and have your child reproduce the sequence.

5. Draw a sequence of shapes, numbers, or letters. Cover and have your child draw an identical sequence. Begin with two shapes.

6. Play concentration card games. Use four pairs of identical cards to start. Lay cards down face up and have your child observe their position, then turn them face down and have him try to find matching pairs. Increase the number of cards as your child becomes more proficient.

V. <u>Auditory Memory</u> is the skill involved in repeating a sentence or a grocery list. To remember a series of verbal directions given by the teacher, the child must have developed his auditory memory.

<u>Task 5</u> - Repeating digits. Basic skills involved: auditory memory, concentration.

Tell your child you're going to ask him to repeat some numbers after you. Then say the number "three" twice, and wait for him to respond, correcting him if necessary. "Now say, 2, 6." When your child understands the task, proceed to the exercise items.

1. 3-6
2. 4-2
3. 7-1-3
4. 4-9-5
5. 2-7-6-3
6. 5-9-4-7
7. 4-2-5-9-6
8. 5-7-4-2-9

Expected performance:
Kindergarten, 7 correct
First grade, all correct

<u>Auditory Memory Activities</u>

1. Have your child repeat increasingly long sentences.
2. Give him a series of directions such as "turn around, jump, clap your hands three times, and walk to the door."
3. Help your child memorize simple rhymes or songs.
4. Add practice in motor activities by putting letters or numbers on the floor with chalk or masking tape, and telling him a sequence to either hop or bounce a ball on.

VI. Concentrating and Paying Attention is necessary for early school sucess. How long can the child sit and work on a puzzle or look at a book? How easily is he distracted from his task by other sounds or activities in the room? Will he need the teacher by his side to focus his attention on his work or will he be able to maintain his concentration independently?

Task 6 - A child entering kindergarten should have been able to do the preceding tasks in one sitting without having become too fidgety or tired. He should also be able to give each task sustained attention until completion. If your child falls short of this performance, however, do remember that so do a great many other children. If his exercise scores are lower than those cited, or his attention wanders, remember that anyone's level of performance varies from time to time, as does his willingness to pay attention to the job at hand. So don't worry; but do follow through with the remedial games.

Attention and Concentration Activities

All of the preceding tasks require some degree of concentration and attention. Begin with very short sessions (one or two minutes if necessary) and gradually increase their length as he becomes familiar with the procedure.

VII. Self-Image - All of our perceptions emanate from ourselves. If your child does not know what he looks like or where he is in space, he cannot relate to other objects around him. A child who bumps into a doorjamb or falls over someone's feet is not necessarily careless or clumsy. If that child doesn't have a concept of his own size or how much space he takes up, he does not know how much room to allow himself in order to get through a doorway or around someone's feet. To further explain the statement that we perceive everything from the viewpoint of our own body in space, consider the fact that if you are facing one way in a room, what you call the right side of the room is to your right. But to someone facing you, the other side of the room is the right side.

Self-Image Activities

1. When helping a small child bathe, name the parts of the body as they are washed.

2. Name the parts of the body as clothes are being put on: for example, stockings go over the toes, foot (arch and heel), ankle, calf, knee, and so on. If the child could look in a mirror while this is being done, it would be helpful.

3. In going to the grocery store, church, or the like, point out special landmarks: filling station by name, big red house, a bank by name, or whatever outstanding landmark you can find. Call attention to distances: "There's the Texaco gas station. Now we are two blocks from home." Or, "Now we have three blocks to go to get to the store."

4. As a child gets close to school age, draw a simple map between home and some other location not too far away; have corners to turn, right and left. Let the child take the map and guide you in the car or walking to the destination on the map.

5. Keep a "growing" record on the wall somewhere, so that the child can see how much he has grown.

6. Compare the clothes he wore when he was smaller with what he presently wears, so that he can get some idea of how long his arms are getting, for instance.

7. Let him compare clothes of a younger or older brother or sister to help him understand where he is according to size.

8. Let him help decide what size pitcher or dish to put something into. If he chooses incorrectly, don't say so, but show him by going ahead and putting whatever it is in the pitcher or dish. He will quickly understand why the container is too small or too large.

VIII. Vocabulary - This skill involves understanding and using a sufficient number of words so as to communicate his thoughts, feelings and wants. It also involves the ability to draw meaning from what is being said to him.

Vocabulary Activities

Talking to a child, holding a conversation in which he is involved-is just about the best way to help him develop a vocabulary. In other words, you need to talk with your child, not at him. The following are some specific things you can do to help him:

1. We will start again in the kitchen. So many words can be taught right in connection with kitchen activities: for instance, such words as beating, stirring, measuring, creaming, thickening, chopping, dicing, tenderizing, cutting, paring, hulling, snapping, grating, mashing, whipping, marinating. The kitchen is the logical place to learn the difference between such words as crisp and chewy, spicy and bland, sweet and sour, hot and warm, cold and cool, rare and well-done, fried and broiled, steamed and boiled.

2. Parents can begin early to train their child in the sequencing of the alphabet and the beginning sound each letter makes. Have the child pick up or put away his toys alphabetically: "A" toys, "B" toys, and so on. Have him name each toy as he puts it away. Say each word with him, accentuating the beginning sound. You could have "A" day-all toys starting with A put away first; "D" day-all toys starting with D would be first.

3. Give him the letters of the alphabet on cards made out of sandpaper or flannel, or alphabet blocks. Sit him down with a newspaper, preferably full-page ads because the letters are larger. Give him colors and let him circle all A's in red, all B's in blue, and so forth. Use just two or three letters at a time. This activity will keep him busy for some time.

4. Of course, there is nothing that can compare with reading aloud to a child. Nursery rhymes, rhyming words, short poems with repeated lines the child can say along with you-all are excellent. Reading aloud helps build listening skills, and an interest in wanting to read for himself later on.

5. When talking to your child, give names of things, Don't just say, "Here, take this." Say, "This is a cup. Will you hold the cup, please?"

6. Name things and read signs aloud as you go down the street, or as you look at a book or magazine.

Conclusion

By becoming proficient in the basic skills we have explored here, your childs' overall development should progress.

A parent's function is no different than that of a teacher. Teaching the child many essential skills requires specific time for training and instruction. These skills cannot always be accomplished through incidental comments. A conforming, cooperative child may learn all the necessary rules by observation, but if the spontaneous process of learning doesn't take place, special instruction is necessary. How to eat, how to dress, how to cross a street, and similar performances should be taken up one at a time in a consistent routine until each is learned in a positive setting.

Everyday find some little thing to give your child praise for-even if it is just for trying. And every day remember to touch your child, to give him a quick hug, a pat on the head, a smile or a wink meant just for him. In other words, give him love.

REFERENCES

Arnold, Your Child's Play
Simon & Schuster, Inc.
630 Fifth Avenue, N.Y., N.Y. 10020

Behrman & Millman, How Many Spoons Make A Family?
Academic Therapy Publications
1539 Fourth Street, San Rafael, Calif. 94901
$2.00

Ceddine, Anthony, A Parent's Guide To School Readiness
Academic Therapy Publications
1539 Fourth Street , San Rafael, Calif. 94901

Getman, G.N., How To Develop Your Child's Intelligence
Research Publications
544 Richards Road, Wayne, Penn., 19087
$4.50

Gordon, Gurough, & Jester, Child Learning Through Child Play
St. Martin's Press, Inc.
175 Fifth Avenue, N.Y., N.Y. 10010
$3.95

Members of the Staff of the Boston's Children's Medical Center, and Gregg, E. What To Do When There Is Nothing To Do
Dell Publishing Co.
1 Dag Hammarskjold Plaza, N.Y., N.Y., 10017
$.95

Miller, Julano, Helping Your L.D. Child At Home
Academic Therapy Publications
1539 Fourth Street, San Rafael, Calif. 94901
$2.50

U.S. Government Printing Office, Your Child From One To Six
Washington D.C.

Evaluating Children's Progress
Day Care and Child Development Council of America, Inc.
1012 14th Street, N.W. Washington D.C., 20005
$3.50

Friends of Perry Nursery School, The Scrap Book
Perry Nursery School
1541 Washtenaw Avenue, Ann Arbor, Mi., 48104
$2.50

Step Six

Know How to Read a Textbook

When you know how to read a textbook, you comprehend and remember what you read.

Textbook authors have already done a lot of your work for you. They've inserted boldfaced subtitles that tell you exactly what you are going to be reading about. They've put all of the important words in **bold** or *italic* print, and they've added pictures, charts, graphs, lists of vocabulary words, summaries, and review questions. The textbook authors have done all of this to make it easier for you to learn and retain the information they're presenting.

In this section, you will discover how to use these "learning tools." You'll also learn how to **1) Scan**, **2) Read**, and **3) Review**. Once you know how to scan, read, and review, you will be able to comprehend and remember what you read the first time through.

Scan. Scanning gives you a quick overview of the material you're going to read. To scan, read the title, the subtitles, and everything in bold and italic print. Look at the pictures, graphs, and charts, go over the review questions, and read the summaries.

On the following page you'll find an article about the Beatles taken from a music history textbook. If you were to scan the page, you would read the title, **The Beatles**, and each of the section headings: **The Beatles dominate the music industry**, **The Beatles get start in Liverpool**, **The Beatles change their image**, **The Beatles find success in U.S.**, and **The Beatles go their separate ways**. You would read everything in bold print (**Paul McCartney**, **Ringo Starr**, **George Harrison**, **John Lennon**, **Brian Epstein**, and **Rock and Roll Hall of Fame**), you would look at the *"Best Selling Beatles' Albums"* chart, and you would read the review questions.

Scanning provides you with a great deal of information in a very short amount of time. (Look at how much you learned about The Beatles just from reading the section headings.) In addition to providing you with an excellent overview of the material, scanning also provides you with a kind of "information framework." Having this framework of main ideas, vocabulary words, etc. makes it easier for you to read, understand, and remember the more detailed information.

The Beatles

The Beatles dominate the music industry.

The Beatles were a British rock group that dominated the rock and roll industry from 1958-1970. The Beatles had an enormous impact on music and were the single most important component in the creation of the modern day "pop" culture. The members of the group, **Paul McCartney**, **Ringo Starr**, **George Harrison** and **John Lennon** had a synergistic effect on each other musically. Their playful, yet irreverent public image captured the imagination of an entire generation.

The Beatles get start in Liverpool.

In the summer of 1957, John Lennon and Paul McCartney began playing together in Liverpool, England. Later that year Paul invited guitar player George Harrison to join the group. The band was becoming popular around the area when they were booked to play a series of concerts in Hamburg, Germany. The group honed their musical skills in the Hamburg beerhalls, playing a repertoire of standard American rock and roll songs.

The Beatles change their image.

On returning from Hamburg, they were discovered by **Brian Epstein**. He became their manager and he changed the image of the band, exchanging black leather jackets and tight jeans for collarless suits and slightly androgynous haircuts. In May of 1962, Epstein landed the Beatles their first recording contract. Shortly before entering the studio, drummer Ringo Starr was added to the group. The early Beatle recordings were instantly successful and soon the band was headlining tours.

The Beatles find success in U.S.

In 1964 the Beatles' music was released in the United States. The sales were tremendous, breaking all previous records. The band came to New York in April where screaming fans met them at the airport, and 70 million people watched them on the *Ed Sullivan Show*. Throughout the 60's the Beatles' popularity grew. Their 1967 album *Sgt. Peppers Lonely Hearts Club Band* was released to unprecedented critical acclaim. A series of artistically creative and commercially successful albums followed.

The Beatles go their separate ways.

By the end of 1968 the members of the group had begun to go in different directions. Paul McCartney continued to write "pop" melodies while George Harrison immersed himself in eastern spirituality. John Lennon grew more distant from the band as he grew closer to his wife, Yoko Ono. In April of 1970, McCartney released his first solo album and announced the end of the Beatles.

Throughout the 70's the Beatles' music continued to be popular, and they were constantly hounded to reunite. Lennon's murder by a mentally deranged fan in December of 1980 ended such speculation. The Beatles were inducted into the **Rock and Roll Hall of Fame** in 1988.

Best Selling Beatles' Albums (in millions)

The White Album	16
Best of 67 - 70	14
Best of 62 - 66	13
Abbey Road	11
Sgt. Pepper	10

Review questions

1.) How many Beatles were there? Which two were the first to play together?
2.) What year did the Beatles start their recording career? When did they break up?
3.) After their break up, did the Beatles ever reunite? Why or why not?

115

Read. When your reading has a purpose, your comprehension improves and it's easier for you to stay focused. To give your reading purpose, try turning each boldfaced subtitle into a question. For example, you could turn the subtitle, **The Beatles change their image**, into the question, "What did The Beatles do to change their image?" Keep your question in mind as you read, and when you finish that section, see if you can answer it. Your question gives you something specific to look for, and it helps keep your mind from wandering. You therefore remember more of what you read.

Friday, April 29, 1994

OPINION

Ypsilanti Press

Recognizing the signs of a problem

As promised, this article will help parents look at the differences between normal adolescence (which some call "hormones on two feet") and adolescence affected by drugs or alcohol.

But first, two important "points."

My husband and I have raised three children. We are certainly not *experts* on mankind's most difficult, complex and absolutely exhilarating undertaking. As a matter of fact, I think we would have *felt* more like experts on the matter of child raising if we had never had any of our own.

I can't imagine for a second how awful it would have been not to ever have known or loved John, Cassandra and Jimmy, but *only* then would we have been in a position to offer other parents "advice" without some fears of reprisal. As typical loving parents, we made many "mistakes" along the way. Hopefully, our kids haven't suffered because of our ignorance, but as wonderful as we think they are, there were times (we're finding out now) that they pulled stunts to which our first response was often, "*My* kid(s)—wouldn't do *that!*" Sound familiar?

Much of what I share with you this week and next will be a distillation of PRIDE "lessons," progressional/personal training or experience and "pieces" of information provided by Birmingham-Bloomfield Families in Action. Having said all that ....

Patricia J. Dignan

Many of the highs and lows teenagers experience are due to their normal physiological changes. It is sometimes difficult for parents to distinguish between such "ups and downs" and those caused by initiation to drug/alcohol experimentation. At this stage, jumping too quickly to conclusions can be just as dangerous as denying there might be something to worry about. Rather than overreact, underact or panic, remember that a *combination* of the following "signs" may be cause for concern:

- Odor of alcohol or unusually heavy use of gum or breath fresheners.
- Heavy use of perfume or after-shave to cover odor of smoke.
- Interest in partying whenever parents aren't around.
- Decreased interest in social activities held at school, church or with family members.
- Morning after fatigue, "grouchies, flu" or unusual thirst.
- Middle of the night vomiting.

Marijuana is extremely difficult to detect because visible effects wear off after an hour or two and there's no lasting odor. Some parents can tell the difference in their child's eyes through lack of alertness, dilation of pupils, avoidance of eye contact, etc. ... strange phone calls, secretiveness or vagueness about activities and whereabouts after school (or frequently finding reasons not to be home even though there aren't specific extra-curricular events) may be additional signs if part of an overall *pattern;* otherwise, these last descriptors could still be confused with "normal" teen-age behaviors.

The teen-age years are those which bridge childhood and adulthood; by definition they are bound to be — at times — "confusing" years for everyone involved. By working closely with the professionals who spend almost as much time with your adolescent as you do (and also have your teen-ager's best interests at heart), schools and families will be able to rely on each other to send consistent and accurate messages to *all* kids that drinking, dangerous drugs and "normal" development don't necessarily go "hand-in-hand."

In my next column, I will suggest signals to watch for which could be indicative of regular use and/or drug dependency among adolescents. I will also list local resources and agencies that help parents answer personal questions.

(Dignan is superintendent of the Milan Area Schools.)

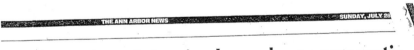

THE ANN ARBOR NEWS SUNDAY, JULY 28

Parents get training in drug abuse preventio

By JOHN A. WOODS
NEWS STAFF REPORTER

Pat McGauly Everett has five children; four will be in Saline schools next year. Her kids aren't on drugs, and she intends to keep it that way.

"There aren't any support groups until you have trouble," she says. "Once you have problems, they are all over the place. We need support groups to help parents prevent problems."

McGauly Everett was one of 15 parents from four local school districts who received basic training in parenting skills and drug abuse prevention at a two-day workshop recently in Ypsilanti.

The Parent to Parent Drug Prevention workshop was led by John Clarkin from the Parent Resource Institute for Drug Education based in Atlanta.

Milan Area Schools Assistant Superintendent Patricia Dignan invited Clarkin to lead the sessions that focused on effective parenting as the key to preventing drug abuse.

Dignan invited parents from Milan, Saline, Ypsilanti and Lincoln schools and convinced each school district to chip in for the $8,500 cost for the training.

After parents are trained as facilitators, they then go out to community groups and share the message.

"What we have done is made it possible for 15 trained people to cut across school district boundaries and provide workshops for three different kinds of parents," Dignan says.

"One kind of parent doesn't know about the problem of kids, drugs and alcohol. The other kind will be one who knows about the problem, but doesn't know what to do about it. And the third kind of parent is one who knows the problem and is already working to prevent it in their own homes."

School buildings are not where kids go to get high. According to a 1988 PRIDE survey of high school students, less than 2 percent of drug use takes place at school. The bad news is the battlefields are located in homes, in cars, at parties and in the street.

Clarkin came to the training session armed with statistics, audio and video tapes and a personal commitment to educating parents. "I've been doing this for two years," he says. "I got involved because my sister had gotten involved with drugs. I didn't want other parents to go through what my parents went through."

The idea behind the program is to focus on parenting skills. "We deal with issues of trust, consequences, punishment and family belief systems," Clarkin says.

Dignan says these days most parents have found themselves confused about issues of right and wrong, and lost in the gray area of being their children's pal rather than parent.

"The days of common community standards and expectations for young people are gone," she says. "So the lines are no longer clear for kids or parents in terms of what's right and wrong. Everything from billboards to TV commercials tell us how to get high... The strength of the program is to form a network of parents to help combat the feeling of powerlessne over the pull of drugs and alcohol in our society."

Steve Porter has a 5-year-old daughter, works as a teacher in Milan and is sold on the idea of parents helping parents. "By setting up the networks you then have a peer group that helps you to confront the peer group that's putting pressure on your kids," he says. "The kids are united; they work together. So should we."

Eddie Kosky, a mother of three sons from Ypsilanti, says the emphasis on awareness struck a chord with her. "I was surprised by a lot of the things we learned," she says. "It was an awareness group. We learned what behaviors you look for in your child. The parenting skills help you recognize attitude changes that may or may not be related to drug use."

The workshops also featured a section on avoiding the mistakes that lead to your child becoming an addict or alcoholic. "By being their banker, their lawyer, their best friend. Not teaching them responsibility. If they get in trouble and you keep bailing them out, you're giving them permission to fail," Dignan says.

By mid-August, all 15 of the new facilitators will meet in Milan to discuss strategy and put their skills to work.

"We want to make this available to any parent," Dignan says. "We don't want this training to just be an event. We want it to be the birth of a process. We will host it in people's homes, in churches, schools, community centers, wherever people are."

For more information, call Dignan at 439-1541.

Parents Can Meet the Challenge Of Raising A Drug-Free Child

By Dr. Patricia J. Dignan

We all know that parents are the first and best teachers of their children, especially from birth through the teen years. Time spent during those years will hold deep payoffs for both parent and child for the rest of their lives.

But when it comes to drugs and alcohol, time together isn't enough. Parents are often silent contributors to their children's journey into the drug culture and thus have to be wary of their own attitudes first.

The obvious ways to counter the wrong attitude or example and influence children positively are to talk to them, act as conscious role models, and bolster self-esteem. Less obvious but as important are the ways we listen and provide non-verbals. A hug goes further than the circumference of two arms, and a parent who is quick to criticize or always offers an opinion may find himself/herself frequently tuned out.

How can parents help their children "tune in" to the dangers of drugs? When is the appropriate moment?

Whenever you both can converse about situations on T.V., or when the natural course of living puts the topic before you--that is a good time to ask and answer questions without lecturing. At those times you can counteract the myths that drinking is cool or macho and always helps people have more fun.

In everyday exchanges, make your child feel important and resourceful. Help your children develop coping skills instead of reasons for copping out. Learn to take your children seriously. If they feel valued at home, they have less need to seek affirmation with undesirable friends.

The following list of "do's and don'ts" might be helpful regardless of the age of your child:

DO

..Praise your child for effort as well as success
..Teach that doing one's best IS winning
..Allow children natural consequences
..Help set realistic, small-piece goals
..Focus on bad behavior, not bad individuals
..Let kids be responsible for things outside self.
..Enjoy the frustrations and fun they bring

DON'T

..Leave liquor around kids or their baby-sitters
..Let them serve alcoholic beverages to adults
..Let them sample your drinks
..Forget to express your love and respect often

The Milan School District is offering one last series of PRIDE training for parents after spring break, in sessions close to your home. The cost is $10 for one parent or $15 for two. Call my office at 439-1541 to sign up now. These classes help with all aspects of parenting and involve 8 hours worth of your time, your most valuable currency. The payoff, however, is priceless.

PRIDE uses an acrostic of PARENT to get its message across:

P Put yourself in the way
A Awareness is your best friend
R Remember the Difference
E Expect and Inspect
N Never cry alone
T Take time for yourself

This last piece of advice is especially important for today's busy parent. Remember, as the mother and father go, so goes the family.

Next week I will tell parents what to look for to determine if their children are experimenting with drugs or just going through "normal" adolescence; sometimes it's difficult to tell the difference.

"Meeting the Challenge"

Dr. Patricia J. Digna

Recently you may have read about the results of a recent Western Michigan University survey Milan youngsters participated in just a few weeks ago. Students in 8th, 10th and 12th grades were asked 53 questions relative to drug and alcohol use among their friends and the students themselves. The results, although shocking, are comparable to those of neighboring districts but well above the national average.

These results should sound an alarm bell in all of us throughout the Ypsilanti area as well because the use of inhalants and marijuana is particularly high. There is also an attitude among marijuana users that there are no long term effects and it's not "as bad" as some other drugs people use. Research is disputing both of those arguments. Marijuana attaches to the body lipids and , when used in large or frequent quantities, stays with the body for as long as 6 weeks. When alcohol's presence can only be detected for 72 hours, that should tell us something about marijuana's insidious nature. Recent studies at the University of Florida have found that neck and head injuries were more prevalent among marijuana users. Researchers also tell us that more times than not marijuana is a gateway drug, the one that opens experimentation with a lot of other drugs and thus should be carefully watched.

These results do not mean that all the kids in Milan and Ypsilanti are smoking pot nor sniffing glue nor speeding off somewhere to get drunk. To the contrary, anyone working with our youth will tell you how refreshing and "clean" most of them are. Milan teens, for example, are very involved in school and community and most are the kind of people any of us would be proud to claim. So why the high results? I'd like to tell you that the results are skewed by our kids bragging and exaggerating but, in good conscience, I can't. Although we know some of that has taken place in a survey of this kind, it would be hard to explain why Milan kids would brag more than seniors around the country.

Does our location have anything to do with these results? Absolutely. Anytime high schools are close to college campuses these kinds of activities are more widespread. And we are in the middle of 2 major universities, 2 large community colleges and a private/business college so the opportunity as well as the mode6ling are there for any teen who wants to access either. I believe that the Ann Arbor penalty of $5.00 does nothing to help kids stop; as a matter of fact, it may just give the message that it's "ok'.

So where do these kids use their drugs? Ironically, the only place in the country where it can be said that any group is "winning the war on drugs" is in our schools. Students and law officials confirm that the incidence in school is almost zero while drug and alcohol useage skyrockets on the weekends and evenings.

Do you know where your kids are? Do you know what to look for when it comes to sniffing out pot or alcohol? Do you want to know more? Milan Area Schools is joining several other schools and organizations to bring Penny Norton, Director of FACE (Facing Alcohol Concerns through Education) to Dexter High School next Thursday, March 24, at 8:00 p.m. This event is free and open to the public in conjunction with March being Parent Awareness Month.

Milan Area Schools will also offer one more series of PRIDE training for parents after spring break. Milan Area Schools took the leadership role in training 16 local (from Milan, Ypsilanti, Lincoln, and Saline) parents/professionals to facilitate this 8 hour inservice program for parents interested in bringing up kids in today's challenging world. As a result, we have trained over 200 parents in Milan and helped train an equal number in Saline in this program which is appropriate no matter what ages your children might be. The cost is $10.00 per person or $15.00 per couple to help defray the cost of workshop materials and we make attempts to locate the sessions close to home and at times most convenient for the participants. If there are 10 or more parents from Ypsilanti, for example, we'd arrange for training to take place there night or day. If you are interested in securing a slot early, call my office at 439-1541.

In the meantime, don't panic; neither should you become smug if you have middle school or high school children. Milan kids are like kids throughout the county--don't think these scores are an aberration or peculiar to Milan. Instead call your school to see if they have done a comparable survey. This problem belongs to all of us. Together we can fight this war on drugs for all kids while you continue to watch out for yours. Next week we'll describe some of the things the schools are doing to change attitudes among kids about drugs and we'll share some pointers for parents.

Article for "Easter Week" from Dr. Patricia J. Dignan

How Parents Can Meet the Challenge of Raising A Drug-Free Child

We all know that parents are the first and best teachers of their children especially from birth through the teen years. Time spent during those years will have deep payoffs for both parent and child for the rest of their lives.

But When it comes to drugs and alcohol, time together isn't enough. Parents are often silent contributors to their children's journey into the drug culture and thus have to be wary of their own attitudes first.

The obvious ways to counter the wrong attitude or example and influence children positively are to talk to them, act as a conscious role model and build their self-esteem. Less obvious but as important, are the ways we listen and provide non-verbals. A hug goes further than the circumference of two arms and a parent who is quick to criticize or always offers an opinion may find himself/herself frequently tuned left alone.

When is a teachable moment? Whenever you both can relax or as situations on t.v. in the natural course of living put the topic before you. At those times you can counteract the myths that drinking is cool or macho and makes people have more fun. Make your child feel important and resourceful. Help your children develop coping skills instead of reasons for copping out. Learn to take your children seriously. If they feel valued at home they have less need to seek affirmation with undesirable friends. Don't always rush in to "save" your son or daughter from an embarrassing moment, frustration or disappointments. Those things, too, are the stuff of life and children need to know how to handle the bad times as well as the good. Otherwise, they'll begin to numb the pain and avoid the maturation that comes through living with predictable lumps and lulls.

Present the right mixture of limits appropriate to their age. Remember medicine can even be toxic if the dosage or the duration is excessive. Children who are able to grow up in an environment with strong and consistent limits develop a sense of security and control. But children who grow up in an overly restrictive home feel they cannot possibly "measure up" and often give up as a result.

The following list of "do's and dont's " might be helpful:

Do

...Praise your child for effort as well as success
...Teach that doing one's best IS winning
...Allow children natural consequences
...Help set realistic, small-piece goals

...Focus on bad behavior, not bad individuals
...Let them be responsible for things outside self
...Enjoy the frustrations and fun they bring

Don't
...Leave liquor around them or their babysitters
...Let them serve alcoholic beverages to adults
/ ..Let them sample your drink
...Forget to express your love and respect often

The Milan School District is offering one last series of Pride training for parents after spring break in sessions close to or in your home if there is enough interest. Call my office at 439-1541 to sign up now.

PRIDE uses an acrostic of parent to get its message across:

P Put yourself in the way
A Awareness is your best friend
R Remember
E Expect and Inspect
N Never cry alone
T take time for yourself.

This last piece of advice is especially important for today's busy family. Take good care of yourself and many of these things will fall into place for you.

MILAN PARENT ENRICHMENT SEMINAR
October 25, 1989

TIPS FOR PARENTS

How to Study a Textbook

1. When the teacher gives an assignment, be sure that you write it down in detail. If you are not sure of it, ask the teacher to explain it further. It is important to have the correct assignment before opening your textbook to study.

2. Read the preface, the introduction and the table of contents. Check the table of contents to determine how your assignment ties in with both past and future lessons.

3. Scan the chapter rapidly at first, just noting the highlights. Make check marks by new words so that they may be looked up later.

4. Read the summary and questions at the ends of the chapter.

5. Read the chapter and do the following:

   a. List all new words, look them up in a dictionary and write the definitions and synonyms for them. Reread the sentences using the words in context.

   b. Put new words, definitions, important details and technical terms on flash cards, which can be studied whenever you have a few extra minutes between classes or at any other convenient time.

   c. Take each main idea and turn it into a question. Divide your notebook page into two parts and write the question on the left side.

   d. When you have finished with the second reading, close your book and answer the questions in your notebook, placing the answers immediately opposite the questions. Answer in your own words; do not use the author's exact words unless you have been told to do so.

   e. After you have provided your answers, open the book and correct incomplete or inaccurate answers.

   f. To review, cover the answers and say the material aloud to yourself. This will use another sense and strengthen the learning.

   g. To strengthen memory, review frequently; distributed review is very important to remembering.

   h. When you think that you really know the material, stop for a few minutes; then spend 10 or 15 minutes more on the material. This can increase your memory of the material remarkably.

6. If your reading is exceptionally heavy and you have a very short time in which to cover a large amount of material, read the main subjects in the chapter very rapidly as they are outlined in the table of contents; then skim through the chapter very rapidly. Read the main points only--the paragraph topic sentences and section headings. Try to tie these materials to the information you obtained from the table of contents.

Studying for Examinations

The following ideas will help you get ready for and successfully complete examinations:

1. Arrange your study schedule so that cramming will not be necessary.
2. Take a calm view of what you need to study. Don't waste time going over material you already know, and don't let yourself become upset by insignificant details.
3. Plan for your final intensive reviewing in the weeks prior to test week and relax the night before you take the test.
4. If you study the night before a test, go to sleep immediately afterward, if possible.
5. Develop speed in answering questions.
6. If you don't know what kind of test you'll have, study as though you were going to have an essay test.
7. Do something besides reviewing during examination week. You need some recreation in order to function efficiently.
8. Keep yourself in good physical and mental condition during examination week. Get enough sleep.
9. Arrive for the test on time, making sure you have adequate materials with which to take the test.
10. Approach the test methodically:
    a. Read and follow all directions carefully.
    b. Look through the whole test, noting the parts that seem most difficult.
    c. Do the easy parts first, as well as the parts that count most, unless you have been instructed to answer the questions in order.
    d. Before you answer a question, read it again to make sure you understand its meaning and implications.
    e. Reject the temptation to guess the answer unless you have an honest basis for believing it to be correct.
    f. Whenever you can do so quickly, associate questions with each other and with as many important ideas as you can develop.
    g. Write legibly; waste no words; waste no time, but do not hurry too much.
11. Reread your paper before you hand it in, making corrections, additions and any changes you find necessary.
12. Remember -- "it's not what you know that earns you grades; it's what you let the instructor know that you know."

Dear Family:

Your children's skills can be challenged and strengthened through the newspaper. This is a brainstormed list of inexpensive uses for some materials found at home. Your children and your own ideas will make this list grow. The time and frequency will depend on those involved.

I. INFORMATION SECTIONS

A. Main Idea - details

B. Sentence structure - Subject (who) - Predicate (what) Nouns (people, places, things) - Verbs (action, feelings)

C. Dictionary

D. Drawing paper - collage

E. Practice spelling words - cut out letters, words found in articles

F. Maps - locations, analyze ledgens

G. Math - advertisements, want ads
1. Shopping - consumer questions, at the store
2. Meal Planning - story problems
3. Graphs - find words to letters in name

II. COMIC STRIPS

A. Sequencing - cut strip - place in order

B. Alphabetical order - titles, authors

C. Nouns/Verbs

D. Cut out speach bubbles - creat own

E. Use character to create own story or comic strip illustrate

F. Ann Arbor News - Sunday Comics - Mini Page

III. T.V. GUIDE

A. Articles

B. Crossword Puzzles

C. Family viewing - attitude adjustment - certain programs permitted during certain times, exchange creative activities for television through positive rewards.

D. Nickelodeon - Mr. Wixard's World

E. P.B.S., Lansing, Toledo, Detroit, 321 Contact, Nova

Your children will also have success with activities at there indivdual levels.

A. Beginning/Ending sounds, vowels

B. Sequencing, listening

C. Alphabetical order

D. Main idea, what do you think?

E. Math

F. Maps - directions

I know you will all benefit by the sharing these activities will promote. Please share your comments and experiences with me.

ACKNOWLEDGEMENTS

This story would not have been one of hope had it not been for hundreds of dedicated teachers at all of my buildings. Woodruff teachers who helped "fight the fight" made that school one of the top 100 schools in the nation despite the terrible conditions we inherited. And the teachers at Chappelle who had struggled for years were overwhelmingly grateful for a lessening of the tension and chaos that had preceded my time there. Although my Ardis teachers were the most challenging both because of strong identification with tradition and paradoxical openness to change, the bottom line in all 3 schools was, whatever it takes, if it makes things better for kids, we'll roll up our sleeves and do it!

Superintendent Ray Barber and Board Members Clyde King, Marcia Harrison, and Tom Manchester buoyed me throughout the trials and tribulations in Ypsilanti, helping me keep my sanity and optimism while Board Members Rose Budd, Roger Ray, Sally Edwards, and Sharon Simechek helped me ensure that Milan Area Schools always met the challenge.

I need to give special acknowledgement to my irreplaceable second hands: Barb Olsen, Linda Baditoi, Marie Williams, Kamille Karlson, Marlou Wiltse, Jackie Bishop, John Milford, and the indomitable Nancy Dugas. These strong loyalists with their sense of humor and compassion along with the following parents were phenomenal: Lucy Butler, Sharon Douglas, and Flora Agnew at Woodruff; Linda Crabtree, Gail Grimes, and Sue Matthews at Chapelle; and Bea Kuwik and Anne Trapani at Ardis, Marilyn Bishop. Special thanks go to Eddie Kosky at West, JoAnn Sheard, and Tom Tobias at Fletcher.

Many exceptional teachers could be counted on to always go the extra mile: Faye Metaj, Warren Ross, Meg Lewandowski, Claudia Ritchie,

Phyllis McDonald, Linda Jamieson, Grace Aaron, Jeanne Swihart, Merrith Sayre, Tulani Smith, Ometha Smith, Kay Brown, Janice Sturdivant, Pat DeRosset, Shirley Lai, Shirley Graessley, Benni Hebrew, Bev Tyler, Connie Williams, Evelyn Finn, Pat Forsburg-Smith, Jovita Davis, Jan Burns, Debra Heyn, John Elliot, Dave Garland, Jim Bush and Paula Fears. My custodians *extraordinaire* Eddie Kubon at Woodruff and Charlie Brown at Ardis proved that for every successful administrator there was always someone behind the scenes making things run smoothly. And Bertha and Dave Provost, Jan Scafasci, and Bev Fanslow (lunch workers) were just the proverbial frosting on the cake!

Credit on systematically creating Expectations for Student Performance goes largely to a corps of middle school and later, high school teachers who helped devise and monitor the processes, especially Jean Richards, Tom Holden, and Carol Reed while I was Assistant Superintendent at Milan. Milan was a system that would have been any administrator's dream: Milan's principals and other personnel were among the most competent and caring I have met.

My family of course, made my long and remarkable career of firsts possible.

My husband, Patrick, was a major (and sometimes, only) source of strength, going to the University of Michigan to take notes on the nights I was giving in-services around the state, then making sure the house and meals were taken care of every weekend so I could be either a law student or a school superintendent without distraction.

Our son, John, and daughter, Cassandra, were wonderful kids who grew into fantastic adults and, ultimately, exceptional educators to carry on the torch. John is a Superintendent and Cassandra is a special education teacher who carries on Jimmy's legacy with awesome devotion to teaching handicapped kids. And then there are my 7 grandchildren who keep me centered and grateful for all of my blessings: Jakob, Lukas, Jonah, and Jayda Coker, and Brendan, Ava, and Siena Dignan, this book is for all of you.

May you each share your amazing gifts with this troubled world you inherited and, despite a scary economy, Covid-19, and riots going on all around you in 2020, turn *your* world into a better place, one filled with love, hope and equal opportunity for all.

ABOUT THE AUTHOR

Patricia Dignan is a woman with many "firsts" in an exceptional administrative career spanning 50 years.

Patricia was the first female Community School Director in the country in 1963, serving in that capacity in Alpena, Michigan, then starting community education in California. She was one of the 1st Head Start Directors under JFK. She was a Director of the 1st Alternative Middle/High School in the country in 1968. She was the 1st female principal in Ypsilanti in the 70's and the 1st (and only) female President of the Ypsilanti Principals' Association. In the 80's she became the 1st female Assistant Superintendent in Monroe County, Michigan, then the 1st female Superintendent in Monroe County in the early 90's. In 1995 in Falls Church, Patricia became the 1st female Superintendent in the greater Washington D.C. area. In 1997, Patricia was named the first Dean of Washtenaw Technical Middle College, the 1st of its kind in the country and which she birthed.

During these years, Patricia pioneered many initiatives and programs. She started the 1st Toy Lending Library in Michigan in the 60's and created the first (and possibly, only) class for parents that included teenagers as resources on parenting in the early 70's. Patricia continued with parenting programs—including a drug-free series of classes—for the entirety of her career.

Patricia opened 7 charter schools in Michigan and oversaw another 12 which featured computer-based learning in the late 90's then became an Executive Director of Student Achievement with Detroit Public Schools where she was responsible for 58 schools over a period of 5 years.

Patricia was also a sought-after national speaker and international consultant during those years. She earned her 1st doctorate at University of Michigan and her 2nd at Detroit College of Law. She has authored 5 books.